The subject of homosexuality is a difficult one for most people to deal with, especially teenagers, who are just finding out who they are in every part of their lives. Using interviews and personal anecdotes along with a historical perspective and scientific information, *When Someone You Know Is Gay* provides a basis for discussion and understanding for teenagers who are straight as well as for those who are not.

SUSAN and DANIEL COHEN are the authors of many nonfiction books for young adults, including *A Six-Pack and a Fake I.D.: Teens Look at the Drinking Question; Teenage Stress;* and *What You Can Believe About Drugs*. The Cohens live in New York State.

When Someone You Know Is Gay

SUSAN AND DANIEL COHEN

Published by
Dell Publishing
a division of
Bantam Doubleday Dell Publishing Group, Inc.
666 Fifth Avenue
New York, New York 10103

To All the Teenagers Who Helped Us Write This Book

ISBN: 0-440-21298-7

RL: 10.1

Reprinted by arrangement with M. Evans and Company, Inc.

Printed in the United States of America

September 1992

10 9 8 7 6 5 4 3 2 1

OPM

Contents

Acknowledgments

The authors would like to thank Parents and Friends of Lesbians and Gays (P-Flag); Gay and Lesbian Youth of New York (GLYNY); Hetrick-Martin Institute; Gay Teachers Association; Oscar Wilde Memorial Bookshop; Sexual Minority Youth League (SMYL); Boston Alliance of Gays and Lesbians; Partners: *The Newsletter for Gay and Lesbian Couples;* Identity House; Dignity: USA; Gay Married Men of New York; New Ways Ministry; Gay Men's Health Crisis; ETVC; The XX (Twenty) Club; Gay Fathers Forum; Faith Temple; Seventh Day Adventist Kinship International; United Methodists for Lesbian and Gay Concerns; The United Fellowship of Metropolitan Community Churches; New Jewish Alliance; and the many others who helped us, most of whom have to remain anonymous.

1   *"I've Got Something to Tell You"*

> "I'm here. You don't have to say hello to me, but I'm here."
>   —BRIDGET Y., AGE 14

> "You always think you're the only one."
>   —ANDY C., AGE 17

What would you do if your best friend came up to you and said, "I've got something to tell you. I'm gay."

Would you stay and talk? Turn away? Walk away? Pretend you didn't hear what you just heard?

Perhaps until the very moment when your friend forced you to confront it, homosexuality seemed distant, a kind of joke, or a kind of a remote menace; something that cropped up in the movies or occasionally on television, a part of life in places like New York's Greenwich Village or San Francisco. It didn't seem to be something that existed in your town—in your school.

Of course it does. Experts estimate that approximately one in ten people are gay. Just as there are gay adults in every walk of life—doctors, factory workers, architects, policemen, farmers, computer programmers, athletes, musicians, secretaries, nurses, teachers, and librarians—so there are gay teenagers in high schools everywhere. Someone your own age that you know is gay.

Let's go back to imagining that right now that someone is your best friend. How you react to your friend's statement will depend on a lot of things, including your personality and your friend's. But unless you are very sophisticated, very tolerant, or very compassionate, you probably won't quite know what to say. Of course, the situation will be a lot easier to handle if you're eighteen and a senior rather than fourteen and a freshman. If you're religious the nature of your religion will affect your attitude; you may consider your gay friend a sinner. You'll probably be influenced by the size of the school you go to. A big school in a cosmopolitan city has a different atmosphere from a small school where everybody knows everybody else and where people have been together in class since kindergarten. Your attitude may also depend on whether your best friend is the same sex you are or a member of the opposite sex. Naturally, the values of your family and community will play a major role.

You sense that what your best friend would like you to say is a cool, calm, "It's okay. Your being gay won't make any difference. We'll still be friends. Nothing will change." But you really can't make that promise. Not if you're disgusted by homosexuality. Not even if you're just surprised, confused, or uncomfortable. Certainly not till you know what being gay is all about.

For instance, does this mean your best friend is attracted to you? For most straight kids that's a scary idea. Where will you rank socially if other people in your school find out? The key to being popular is to have popular friends. Being gay is a social disaster. Who wants to be known as "the faggot's friend"? If you associate with someone known to be gay, won't other people assume you're gay, too? And how about AIDS?

All you've heard about gays are rumors and stories, bits of this and snatches of that. You don't know what's true and what isn't.

Maybe your best friend is mistaken about being gay. After all, he or she has been through all kinds of phases. He or she could just be imagining the whole thing. Though you try to tell yourself this, you know it isn't true. Your friend wouldn't joke about something like this. There's no wishing the problem away. You have to admit to yourself that you are curious about gays, and that if you walk away you won't learn anything further. Of course, you could score points by telling other people your friend's secret. Teens, like grown-ups, love to gossip. Besides, cutting the ties and spreading the story would show other people that you don't hang around with "queers."

But wait a minute. Gay or not, this is still the person who's been fun, who helped you get through chemistry. Telling everybody what you've just learned would make your friend a target. His or her life would be miserable. In high school being different, even in small ways, gets you into trouble with the other kids.

Besides, if hearing your friend is gay is rough, think what your friend is going through telling you. He or she must really need to talk to you or the subject wouldn't have come up. So before you do anything as final as turning away, think a moment. And while you're deciding whether to stay and listen to your best friend or not, let's take a look at the way some gay teens have "come out" or tried to "come out" to their friends and families. ("Coming out" of the closet means first recognizing to oneself that one is gay and accepting it, then telling other people.) Let's start with Tom, who just graduated.

"I was in a car with a group of boys I know well and I said, 'Hey, let's play a kind of game. Everybody, confess a secret.' They told me all kinds of stuff and then I just announced, 'Here's my secret. I'm gay.' Dead silence. Then two of my friends got out of the car. They've never said a word to me since. That hurt. I mean, they were my friends. Two of the others said they didn't care and we stayed friends, but they won't talk about my being gay and they won't let me talk about it, either."

Jennifer, sixteen, says, "Lesbians are invisible to most straight people. I watched a show on television about gay men. It was very compassionate. When's the last time you saw a compassionate show about a lesbian—or any show, come to think of it? You never see much about us at all. Still, hiding is so very painful and being invisible is like not counting as a human being, so I made up my mind I'd come out to my best friend, Peggy. I'd known her since junior high. Then one day I was having lunch in the cafeteria with a group of friends, including Peggy. Somebody started making jokes about gays. Peggy said if she ever found out someone was gay she'd never speak to them again because they might come on to her. I felt like crying. I knew I could never risk talking to her. This fear straight teens have that gays will come on to them is foolish. Gays rarely come on to straight people. We're interested in other gays."

Looking back on the incident, Jennifer feels, "It would have been brave of Peggy to listen, just as it would have been brave of me to tell. It would have meant an opening up, a sharing. It would have been a tribute to our friendship. Instead we just drifted apart."

To Paul, who grew up in a small town in the West and who had known from an early age he was gay, coming out in high school was "unthinkable." "You have to be careful in a small town." Tenth grade was the toughest time for him. "I had the reputation for being pretty weird." Paul's friends were exclusively boys, "nerd types. The jocks wouldn't have anything to do with us." He scarcely knew any girls at all, even though he was in band and chorus and both included a lot of girls. "I know some of my friends suspected I was gay. If only they could have asked me in an honest, friendly way. We could have talked like friends should. But I was too insecure to bring it up. I kept my feelings bottled up inside. People are always watching you, and it's easy to give yourself away."

Paul moved with his mother to a big city in California when he was a junior. Paul found city life liberating. He'd never succeeded in losing himself in a small high school, but in a huge anonymous school he was free to fade into the crowd.

"Better yet, I could find people outside high school I could talk to, straight and gay." At a beach where gays hang out Paul met a college student named John. "He was my first lover. That's when I discovered just how rough it is to be a gay teenager. We couldn't show any affection in most public places, couldn't even hold hands like straight kids. When we went to the movies we'd stand a mile apart from each other in line. I kept thinking it wasn't fair. Still, just to have found someone I could care about and be myself with and who cared about me was the greatest thing to hit me in my whole life."

Candace, who's just turned eighteen, lives in a small city in Indiana. Tall, blond, and as pretty as a model, her looks and feminine style allowed her to hide in high school. On the surface everything seemed to go well for Candace. In reality, life was very difficult.

"Okay, nobody ever hit me or called me names, but I felt terribly isolated. The girls would talk about boys and I couldn't talk about my innermost feelings. I couldn't tell them I was a lesbian. So I used boys as a cover, knowing if I dated boys no one would dream I was romantically attracted to girls. To test myself I had sexual relationships with boys and tried to tell myself I was bisexual. But though the relationships were okay, they weren't what I wanted. Finally I grew so desperate I tried to talk to my older brother when he came home from college. He just wouldn't let me finish, kept saying I was imagining things. It was just an immature phase. It would pass and I'd be 'fine.' "

School is a combat zone to Joshua, whose gestures, voice, and way of walking fit the stereotype of how gay males look and who in fact is gay, something one can't assume just by the way a person looks. "People looking around for someone to hate, the type who like to unload their frustrations on anyone when they can get away with it, pick on me. These are the same kind of people who would beat up the straight black kids in school if they could, but there aren't a lot of black kids in my school." Joshua goes to a wealthy suburban Connecticut high school. "What few blacks there are hang around with each other and protect each other. Nobody'd dare mess with them, anyway. It's not considered acceptable to do that. But it's still okay to take out all your anger on gays."

Recently Joshua made friends with two girls who like him and accept him. Every day at school they stop the boys who bother Joshua and keep them talking until Joshua has a chance to slip past. Unfortunately, they can't help him after school, when the boys often wait for him and beat him up.

Joshua never reports these incidents. After all, he has his pride. He can't turn to his family. His father, a successful businessman, finds Joshua an embarrassment and avoids him by spending all his time at his business. Joshua's mother is an alcoholic, too absorbed in her own problems to recognize his. Besides, Joshua wants to be independent. He also knows perfectly well that if anyone were suspended for beating him up the beatings would begin again —only worse—when that person returned. And there's always the chance Joshua wouldn't be believed, since the most violent incidents occur when no one is around to see.

So even though at seventeen Joshua's bright and articulate and should be headed for college, he's quitting school. He can't concentrate. His marks are low. He sees no reason to spend another full year in "jail." As he says, "The other kids have driven me out. It's really amazing I've made it this far."

If you were to meet Allan, a junior in a New York City high school, you'd think he was a jock and you'd be right. He lives in a working-class neighborhood. His father's a bus driver. His mother works as a waitress. His married sister and her husband and baby live in an apartment down the block. Allan's always gotten along with his parents and he's always had a lot of friends. His biggest struggle has been with himself.

"I tried to be straight. I still go out of my way to be extra macho. You see, I always wanted what my parents want for me. Marriage, kids, that means a lot in our family. It means a lot to me."

In junior high school Allan realized he wasn't attracted to girls. Rather than think about boys, he tried not to think about sex at all. When he couldn't help but think of sex he started buying copies of *Penthouse* and *Playboy*. But he couldn't respond to the pictures.

"I was scared to death the guys would see through my macho pose and call me a 'faggot.' I'd seen what happens to the effeminate kids in school. They're spat upon. I kept telling myself I'd 'cure' myself, but I couldn't. When my friends noticed I was avoiding girls they began wondering why, so I went out with this girl who always talked about how you should wait till you're married to have sex. I also joined in when the guys kidded around with girls, and I pretended I found certain girls sexy. I thought I was covering up well."

Then came an incident Allan will never forget. One Friday night after a football game he went along with his friends to see a girl he knew slightly from school, Meg. Her parents were out. Then, to Allan's total dismay, Meg began flirting like crazy. The guys left them alone together and went into the next room to watch television.

"I was alone with her. I was trapped. The guys expected me to make out with her and they were listening. I was so embarrassed and frightened I did a terrible thing. I lashed out at her, calling her a dog, pretending it was her fault I didn't want to touch her. She believed me and she felt terrible. The guys believed me, too. It was awful of me but it was self-preservation. What could I do? Just a sign I might be gay and I was dead. Nobody wants to be 'the faggot's friend.' Guys I'd known since third grade, guys who'd played football with me through high school, they would have dropped me fast. See why I didn't want to come out to myself?"

As for finding gay friends, "How could I? Where would I meet them? All I've heard of are gay bars where the people are a lot older. Coming out to the whole world, I'm not ready for that. Someday my parents might be able to accept my being gay, but not now. Being gay is supposed to happen, if at all, when you're about twenty. Adults just don't want to believe there are gay kids."

Mary, who goes to a huge city high school, would

include many teachers on the list of adults who
don't want to believe kids can be gay. "Last year
when I was a junior I was discovered in a classroom
kissing another girl. You'd think I'd committed murder. The teacher pounced on us. I got sent to the
principal. All I could think of was, how dare they
treat me like this? What have I done that's so terrible? If I was a boy caught kissing a girl nobody
would have said a word. The only thing that saved
me was the size of the school. On the bus home that
day some boys were talking about how 'a couple of
dykes got caught making out in school' and they had
no idea that one of the girls they were talking about
was me. I was furious. I have a right to privacy like
anybody else."

Like Mary, Tom made his way through high
school by taking risks and being bold, only in his
case most of the time the risks worked. Remember,
it was Tom who announced to a group of friends,
"Here's my secret. I'm gay." Tom wore wild, extreme clothes that drew attention to himself and
contributed to his image as class clown. A good student, he was so popular he was voted student council vice-president. "I used being funny as a way of
warding off trouble. If you can make people laugh
then they won't hit you. They'll even like you."

Of course, not everyone can get away with what
Tom did, and having girlfriends in high school also
helped. "I've always been sexually attracted to girls,
at least enough to cover up being gay. But there's no
tension or excitement for me when I'm with a girl.
From the sixth grade up my fantasies have always
been about boys. After a few dates girls sense that
I'm not really deeply interested in them, that their

relationship with me is different from the relationships they've had with other boys. I like them but call it a feeling of sameness when I'm with them. It's friendship, not love. It's just not right."

When Tom's mother found out he was gay she urged him to see a psychiatrist. "I was fourteen. He tried to change me. I went for a while but then I just told the psychiatrist and my mother I was cured and I quit therapy. I don't believe my sexual identity is something that can be cured or needs to be cured. In the last couple of years my parents have come a long way. They know I'm gay and they've accepted it. They don't hassle me anymore. We've even begun to talk about it."

Candace was afraid to even try to talk to her parents about her homosexual feelings, especially after her brother refused to believe her. Her parents' life was an orderly one that simply didn't allow for the unconventional, the unusual, or the unexpected. The small white house the family lived in was neatly painted, the lawn kept freshly mowed. The family attended church faithfully every Sunday, and Candace's parents firmly believed that their three children, including Candace, were sheltered from the "wickedness" of the world.

Finally Candace met another girl who was agonizing over whether she was a lesbian. "She wrote me a letter. It was just mildly affectionate and friendly, but I hid the letter because I was afraid my parents would literally kick me out of the house if they found it, and where would I go? I became depressed. I was very quiet in school and around the house. Emotionally I was under an awful lot of stress. I kept thinking about how my parents were going to take it when they found out. I had failed them. They had such expectations for me, first college, then marriage, and then children. It would be like the end of the world for them. But you can't hide forever. My mother found the letter and I had to admit the truth. It practically destroyed the family."

Paul's mother, too, found out Paul was gay not because of anything he said but because of a letter. It was a love letter from John, and Paul had left it on top of his aunt's coffee table, maybe accidentally, maybe not. He and his mother were living with his aunt at the time. His mother read the letter and reacted with shock and rage. "How could you do this to me? If only your father were alive he'd know what to do. Somehow he'd know how to get this homosexual stuff out of you. He'd know how to make you change." When Paul's mother told his aunt, his aunt shouted, "What will the neighbors say?"

Paul shouted back, "Who cares?" and his aunt came to a quick and final decision. He'd have to leave her house and go back to the small town he'd come from. His mother didn't argue with his aunt. Paul was given a few weeks to get ready. In those few weeks his aunt did everything in her power to break up Paul's relationship with John.

As the plane took off carrying Paul back to the town he hated, he told himself that in a couple of years he'd be out of high school and then nobody would dare treat him like this again.

Dave, sixteen, is black and Hispanic and grew up in a project in Chicago. "I told my mother I was gay two months ago and she started crying. She blamed herself. She's calmed down now but she won't let me tell my father, and I don't want to. He couldn't handle it. I told my three sisters. At first, they wouldn't believe it. I don't look effeminate. I've tried hard to look real masculine. Girls call me up all the time."

Telling his mother gave Dave a sense of freedom. "I felt like I'd opened up an old trunk and let all the birds fly out and got rid of the spider webs."

High school has been lonely for Dave. "I didn't know anything about the gay life-style. I didn't exactly know what being gay was. I dated girls just to keep up the right image. But they know when you're a phony. I tried to get in with the tough macho guys in my neighborhood. They didn't beat me up or anything like that, but they just wouldn't let me hang out with them. They seemed to sense I was different. I really came out to myself about a year ago.

"For a cover I joined the Jehovah's Witnesses. That sounds like a terrible thing to do, using a religion for cover, but I knew the Witnesses don't believe in your having sex until you're married, and the religion protected me. At school everybody would say, 'Oh, Dave, he's real real moral,' instead of 'Oh, Dave, he's a real fag.' I needed all the help I could get."

Dave was in sixth grade when he first realized he was gay. He couldn't stand the discovery. "Every day I'd take a glass of Kool-Aid, go out on the roof of the project alone, and say, 'God, please turn this into a magic potion that will make me straight.' I'd drink the Kool-Aid but nothing would happen. I'd still be gay. Things are better now, though. I go to a gay youth group and I've got gay friends. Without the youth group there'd be nothing but the bars for gay kids, and that's not the kind of life I want. My biggest fear right now is AIDS. I worry about it and I worry about what AIDS does to straight people, how it makes them scared of being around gays."

Is coming out always traumatic? It doesn't have to be. Meet Jeff, seventeen, who lives in California. "My mother's French, and French people have a different attitude toward sex than Americans. More relaxed. Maybe that's why coming out to myself was so easy. My father's not as relaxed about sex as my mother, but he's always encouraged me to think freely. Prejudice of any kind just wasn't tolerated in my family. I told my mother I was gay a few months ago. She was surprised. She said she didn't know much about homosexuality but if I would give her something to read she'd try to understand it.

"So I went to a gay bookstore and picked up some books for her. After she read them she told my father I was gay. I had a long talk with him about it. Since then he's been very supportive. So have my brothers and sisters. Even my grandmother in France has been terrific. She's going to be on a French radio program talking about gay rights."

These experiences are all different because gays and lesbians are all individuals. Sometimes, because teenage gays are so isolated from the straight world, we who live in that world see them as stereotypes. We tend to lump them together because of their sexual orientation, forgetting that they are total people, just as we are. Though we call ourselves "heterosexuals," we don't think of ourselves as only sexual, and neither do they. One reason gays object to the word "homosexual"—even though they often use the word themselves—is its narrow focus. It emphasizes the differences between "us" and "them" instead of the similarities. When we concentrate on differences, we often feel uncomfortable with gays; even the most sympathetic among us will avert his or her eyes, preferring to shrink back rather than meet them as fellow human beings.

(A brief pause here to clear up some confusion about terminology. The origins of the word *gay* to describe persons attracted to the same sex are obscure and controversial. Technically, the term can apply to either males or females with same-sex attraction, but commonly *gay* refers to males. Females are usually called *lesbians*. Gays and lesbians have been called many names throughout history, most of them insulting. But now there is a new assertiveness among many in the homosexual community. One of the most active gay groups of the 1990s calls itself Queer Nation. Queer was one of the worst things a gay person could be called. But now some have turned the insult around and wear it as a badge of pride.)

Most of us—young people and adults alike—know very little about homosexuals and homosexuality. And a lot of what we think we know is probably wrong. In the next chapter we are going to answer some of the questions you might ask.

2
Is It Catching? and Other Questions You Would Be Too Embarrassed to Ask

"I don't lisp or wear pink or swing my arms when I walk and I like sports. I'm gay."
—JIM D., AGE 17

"I was dreaming about women twenty-four hours a day but I kept telling myself I wasn't gay."
—LAURA P., AGE 15

Is it catching?

No. People who think that somebody can turn gay or be made gay by somebody else are misinformed. Sexual preference comes from within. Outside influences have very little to do with it. So if you're afraid that being around gays or having a gay friend will make you gay, relax. You won't become gay. Just remember, this works both ways. Don't think you can convert your gay friend into being straight. We're not talking about a head cold here. He or she can't catch your heterosexuality any more than you can catch his or her homosexuality.

Can it be cured?

Here we go with the head cold again. Words like "catching" and "cure" are meant for communicable diseases. (We know, we know, you're thinking AIDS. We'll get to that later. Please don't confuse having gay feelings with having AIDS.) Homosexuality is almost impossible to change. The reason we say almost is that there are people who claim they have changed from gay to straight, thanks to therapy or a religious conversion, or for no reason at all. But there is no way to know whether these people have really changed for good, are denying their homosexuality, or were never really gay in the first place.

The evidence is overwhelming that the vast majority of gay people can't change their sexual preference no matter what they do and no matter what is done to them. Over the years gays have been tortured and imprisoned, been given electroshock treatments, psychoanalysis, and hormone injections, and been prayed for. Nothing worked. They remained gay. You can make someone miserable but you can't make them straight.

Is it a choice?

People do not choose to be gay any more than
people choose to be straight. It just happens. By the
way, most gay people find it very insulting that
straight people think they should change. Homosexuality feels natural and comfortable to them. Most
like being gay. When gays hide or fight their innermost feelings it's because they're afraid they'll be
persecuted for being different, not because they
mind finding members of their own sex exciting and
lovable.

What causes homosexuality?

Nobody really knows, though there have been
umpteen theories ranging from glandular imbalances to strong mothers and weak fathers. All the
obvious environmental theories have been discred-
ited. That's because homosexuality has existed since
history began. Gays are found in every racial, religious, and ethnic group, in every culture, in all
kinds of societies from democracies to totalitarian
states, from the most modern nation to the most
primitive tribe. Because homosexuality is so widespread and persistent, most experts don't believe it's
caused by environmental factors like family relationships. Some suspect it's inborn. Whatever its
cause, it's beyond an individual's conscious control.

If I'm the friend of somebody gay, won't everybody think I'm gay, too?

Not everybody, but we won't lie to you. Some people will. We understand what you're worried about.

You've probably noticed how badly teens thought to be gay are treated in your school, and you're afraid that if people think you're gay you'll be hassled, too. You probably also feel you'll be a lot less popular just for being friends with someone gay—or someone everyone suspects is gay.

The hardest time to deal with this is in junior high and in the first two years of high school because that's when everybody dreams of getting into the top clique, worries about being different, worries about having zits, fears being considered a nerd or weird, and can't help falling in love with a new person every three days. You have so much going on inside you during these years that it may be asking too much to expect you to think about what someone else is going through.

Yet the teenager tagged a "fag" has it much rougher than you—at least at school—no matter what you're going through. If you're strong enough to become or remain this person's friend, great. You're on your way to becoming a very special kind of person, loyal and tolerant. Lots of people will be glad to have a friend like you in the years to come. If you can't face being the friend of a gay person now, at least don't become an enemy. Don't join in when people shout insults. Don't make fun of him or her. Say hello when you pass in the halls. Remember, gays are human. Not hurting people's feelings, not making things worse for them, is a gesture of friendship, too.

If you're a junior or senior in high school it's different. You're past the "I can't wear purple if everyone else wears green" and the "If I'm caught with the wrong people at the wrong table in the school cafeteria I may just as well move to another planet" stage. You're at the point in life where your friends should be there for you when you need them and you should be there for them when they need you. Do you really want to be the kind of person who drops somebody, straight or gay, because of what somebody else says or might think? If you are, what excuse will you find to drop the next friend who becomes inconvenient? Imagine how you'd feel if somebody decided to abandon you.

How do they "do it"?

Some straight people think that homosexuality is perverted and pornographic and that gay people can only enjoy sex if they use bizarre sex toys. Frankly, that's ridiculous. Gay sex is natural for gay people, and they do many of the same things straight people do, using the same parts of the body to do them with.

Let's get specific. Gay males kiss, hug each other, touch each other, engage in mutual masturbation, anal sex, and oral sex. Not all gay males do all these things, any more than all straight people do all these things. And they don't do any one thing all of the time.

Gay women—lesbians—kiss, hug each other, touch each other's breasts, touch each other's vagina and clitoris with their tongue and fingers, and lie one on top of the other, enjoying the friction of one body on another. Again, not all lesbians do all these things and, like straight people, they don't always do the same things the same way all the time.

*In a gay relationship is one person always active
and the other passive? Does one partner always
play the "male" role and the other the "female"
role?*

The answer is no. Nowadays gay people take
turns being active or passive depending on their
mood. Actually, the idea of a dominant "male" role
versus a passive "female" role is an outdated con-
cept that doesn't apply to most relationships anymore, whether straight or gay.

*Doesn't a female need penis/vagina intercourse to
achieve an orgasm?*

The part of a woman's body where she experiences orgasm is the clitoris, not the vagina, and lesbians are able to bring each other to orgasm
through mutual masturbation and oral sex. Just as
many straight people think the right woman can
"cure" a male homosexual, so many straight people
also think a sexual relationship with a supermacho
male will "cure" a lesbian of her homosexuality.
What that's really saying is that straight sex is so
wonderful no one could resist it. Well, it is wonderful for straight people, but gay people feel differently. Besides, sexual preference doesn't just depend on physical sex. It has a lot to do with
emotional needs, who we're comfortable with, and
who we can love.

Isn't all this disgusting?

Disgusting? It may seem so to you, but it doesn't disgust gays in the least. Quite the contrary. Not only does it feel right for them but it can be romantic and beautiful. Like straight people, gay people, too, fall in love.

Sometimes straight people focus so much on the sexuality of gays they don't see them as total human beings. Next time you meet a gay person, try to evaluate him or her as you would anyone else. Is the person fun? Does he or she seem nice? Is he or she struggling with math class, too? Do you like the same sports, the same rock groups? Don't worry about what this person does or doesn't do in bed. You don't ask yourself whether every straight person you meet does things you approve of sexually in private. Why ask it about gays? Whatever gays do or just dream of doing (gay teens, like straight teens, are not necessarily sexually active) is their business just as what you do or just dream of doing sexually is your business. The one thing we think is really disgusting is violence. Nobody, gay or straight, should ever be forced or talked into doing anything sexually that they don't want to do. And we mean anything, beginning with a kiss.

What should I do if a gay person comes on to me?

It depends. If you were standing on a New York City subway station platform at night or on a lonely country road and a gay person holding a knife tried to attack you, you'd have every reason to be scared out of your wits. Unfortunately, many straight people react to even the mildest encounter with a gay person as if they were facing a crazy rapist. Some macho-type straight males enjoy bragging about how they "beat up a faggot" who tried to pick them up. Who was the real victim here, the straight guy who was never touched, or the gay guy who was beaten up?

The myth that gay people have an overpowering passion for straight people is just that, a myth. Gays generally gravitate toward other gays. Often gays are accused of coming on to straights when they really haven't. Someone was just looking for an excuse to beat them up. Gay bashing, it's called. Gay bashing can mean verbal abuse as well as physical abuse.

If a gay teenager—say someone at school—expresses interest in you, don't panic. You're not facing an irrational, out-of-control maniac. You don't become violent if someone straight you're not interested in is interested in you, and you know how to say no nicely. Treat the gay teenager the same way. Believe us, the gay teenager is probably a lot more scared than you are. Nobody likes to be bashed.

How can they tell? How do they know they're gay?

Gay people sometimes take this question, turn it around, and ask the rest of us: "How do you know you're straight?" You know you're straight because you can't keep your eyes off good-looking members of the opposite sex. You get crushes on movie stars of the opposite sex. Browsing through magazines filled with erotic pictures of the opposite sex is a turn-on. You fall so in love with a member of the opposite sex in English class that you can't concentrate on your studies. At night you dream about someone of the opposite sex you find attractive. Gays experience all this too, but in relation to their own sex, not the opposite.

Being straight, you do have an advantage. There are many signposts along the way for you. When you go to the movies or watch television you always see male and female couples. At school and on the street it's boyfriends and girlfriends you see holding hands or hugging and kissing. Go to the bookstore and the shelves are filled with books about straight love.

Gay teens don't have signposts. Since homosexuality is a taboo subject in most communities—hidden, covered up, and swept out of sight—gay role models are few and far between. Gay teens are often confused and even frightened by what they feel because no one else seems to share their feelings. They know they're not sending and receiving the same signals their straight friends are. They know their deepest, most consistent, most persistent fantasies are different: homosexual, not heterosexual. But often a gay teen isn't sure exactly what this means, and it may take him or her a while to put a name to it. Besides, like straight teens, gay teens have heard mostly bad things about homosexuality. It's hardly surprising they may be reluctant to say to themselves, "I'm gay."

At what age do people know they're gay?

It varies a lot, but some know as early as childhood. Most know by early to late adolescence. Of course, knowing is one thing and coming out of the closet—that is, admitting their sexual preference to themselves and others—is another. Some gays try to keep their homosexuality a secret even from themselves and don't come out till much later in life.

The idea that someone may be gay as young as twelve or thirteen frightens many straight people who would prefer to think of homosexuality as a choice made voluntarily by adults. That's why young gays are often told that what they're feeling will pass, that it's just a phase. For some kids it may be a phase. Even an occasional homosexual experience doesn't mean one's gay or make one gay, and even the straightest of straights sometimes feels attracted to someone of his or her own sex or has a homosexual dream or fantasy. But for the gay teen homosexuality is not a passing phase he or she will outgrow. It is essential, basic, and deep-rooted.

Do gay teenagers sometimes think they're bisexual?

Many gay teenagers, confused, ill informed, and scared of the stigma placed on homosexuality by the straight majority, do tell themselves they're bisexual. It's a comforting label because a lot of straight people consider bisexuality less drastic than homosexuality. Of course, most people have a very fuzzy idea of exactly what bisexuality is, and even experts disagree. But it sounds better than homosexuality— kind of adventurous and sort of forgivable. You don't hear of people setting out to go "bi bashing" very often.

Besides being a safer thing to admit to, bisexuality allows the gay teen to hold on to the belief of a traditional future of marriage and family. Now, there are gays who marry straights and have children and there are gays who have sex with straights and have children, but these are not the conventional relationships most people are raised to expect. It's hard to abandon the dream of a conventional future. Part of the process of coming out for a gay teen is letting go of the security blanket bisexuality seems to offer and saying to oneself, "I'm not straight, not bi, I am gay." However, a gay teen might continue to tell straight friends and relatives he or she is bisexual. It's a way of testing, of finding out how tolerant people are. The friend who's upset by bi will probably be traumatized by gay. Telling others that one is bisexual is also a way of avoiding the hassles that come from being pegged as gay.

How many people are gay?

It's hard to say because there are still a lot of gay people in the closet. How do you count them? And you can't include only sexually active homosexuals as gay. What about celibate gays—people who are attracted to members of their own sex but don't have sexual relations with anyone? Take celibate gays in religious orders, for example.

Yet based on studies and research projects, experts estimate that about 10 percent of the total population is gay. One in ten is a sizable minority. Put another way, about one of every four families has a gay member. But would we be any more justified in beating up gays, making fun of them, and rejecting them if they were only one in twenty?

What cities do gays live in?

Gays have a saying, "We are everywhere," and it's true. Some cosmopolitan cities, such as New York, San Francisco, and Miami, have large communities of gays. Seattle has a large lesbian population. Gay adults are drawn to these cities because they want to live openly and freely. But don't kid yourself. Gays live in every city, in every suburb, in small towns, and on farms. There are people growing up gay in all fifty states. They come from rich families, middle-class families, and poor families. Some will eventually move to big cities in search of a better life, but many will remain where they are.

Straight people like to wish gays away. If they all lived in Greenwich Village then they'd be somebody else's problem, not ours. We could tell ourselves they don't really exist—not around here, anyway. But whether you see them or not, they're there, living right near you.

Is it a sin?

Most mainstream religions in America do consider homosexual activity sinful. But some do not. Many gay people are highly moral, concerned about ethical questions, deeply religious, and attend church or synagogue regularly. Some refrain from sexual activity. Most are sexually active. Many gays work within established churches or religious organizations, trying to change them. Some have left and gone on to join or establish religious institutions that do not view homosexuality as a sin.

Is it a crime?

Some states have anti-sodomy laws on the books, but they are rarely enforced against consenting adults. Rarely, however, is not the same as never. To gays these laws are a constant threat, a weapon that can always be used against them. Some cities have passed laws prohibiting discrimination against gays. Such laws usually become emotional political issues. In 1991 Governor Pete Wilson of California refused to sign a gay rights bill that initially he had favored. He was accused of caving in to pressures from conservative religious and political groups. The governor's action provoked angry and sometimes violent demonstrations by gay activists. In some places gay rights legislation has been passed and then reversed in a referendum. In California, however, polls indicated that the public actually favored the bill. And just for the record, there are lawyers, judges, police officers, and politicians who are gay.

Can gays marry each other?

Not legally. But some gays who feel they belong together have symbolic wedding ceremonies and because they love each other they consider the ceremony binding. Gay couples may stay together for many years, even a whole lifetime, yet society doesn't acknowledge their relationship. On a practical basis this creates real difficulties for gays. When it comes to insurance policies, mortgages, joint ownership, inheritance, government benefits, etc., gay couples do not have the same rights as legally married couples. No matter how devoted to each other they are, at best the world sees them as separate strangers. There have been moves in some communities, particularly cities with large and politically active gay populations, to grant legal recognition to gay couples, but progress in this area has been slow. One large computer corporation has offered gay couples the same sort of rights as far as insurance and other benefits that it gives to its married heterosexual employees.

Do gays have children?

There is nothing wrong with the reproductive systems of gays, and just as straight people want families so do gays. It may surprise you to learn that many gays get married. Why? Well, there's the lure of a secure family life. Or a gay person may care for one particular straight person. Sometimes gays marry because they're not out to themselves or they think marriage will "cure" them.

When gays marry to hide, it usually doesn't work and the marriage ends in divorce. Even when gays care deeply about their straight partner (and enjoy sex with that partner) they will usually feel that something is missing. Some may seek out gay sexual encounters or have a long-term gay relationship while they're still married. Marriage does not make a gay person straight.

Not all gays who want to be parents marry. A gay man and a lesbian may decide to have a child. Or the gay person may have a sexual relationship with a straight friend of the opposite sex. Unmarried gays often approach parenthood seriously and thoughtfully, and just as they're capable of having children they're capable of loving them, too.

Should gays be allowed to raise children? Won't they make the children gay?

A parent's sexual preference does not determine his or her child's sexual preference. If that's how things worked there'd be a lot fewer gays around, because most gays have straight parents. Gays usually have straight grandparents and brothers and sisters who are straight, and by and large straight people teach them at school. They spend time in classrooms filled with straight kids and play with straight kids after school. Though absolutely drowning in contacts with straight people they still grow up gay.

Most children born to gay parents grow up straight. Even when a child is raised by a gay parent living with a gay partner of the same sex, the homosexual adult relationship will not make the child gay.

There is also no evidence to support the widely held belief that because a person is gay he or she will automatically be a bad parent. There are kind, loving, responsible gay parents just as there are kind, loving, responsible straight parents. And just as there are neglectful straight parents there are neglectful gay parents, too.

Straight people who assume that gay people are automatically a bad or even dangerous influence on the young get very edgy at the mere idea of gays being around children, much less having any. Some even believe gays "got that way" because they were sexually abused by someone of their own sex when they were children. People who hold this belief often think all gays, or at least all gay males, are potential child molesters, perverted, sex-mad vampirelike creatures running around abusing innocent little children and turning them into sexual vampires who will grow up to assault the next generation of children.

Vampires belong in fiction. In reality, 90 percent of all sexual child abuse in the United States is committed by heterosexual men. The victims are almost always girls. Rarely is the girl abused by a stranger. Usually the child is battered or sexually attacked by a close relative or someone she knows. When a child is sexually molested (whether by a straight or gay person), it's a traumatic experience. It is not a turn-on. People who believe that homosexual sex is so much better than heterosexual sex that a gay assault will transform even a terrified child victim into a gay fanatic ought to ask themselves why they think so little of straight sex.

The real problems facing the children of gays are a lot more mundane. They're also universal. The children of gays, like many children of straights, must often cope with divorce. What makes their situation special is that in a parental tug-of-war over custody, a parent's homosexuality can become an issue. Courts are often very tough on gay parents.

When one parent is gay his or her homosexuality can become the focus of a lot of resentment, anger, fear, and blame—especially from the straight parent. Even when emotions cool after the divorce it may take the children of a gay parent time to accept the gay parent's partner, particularly if the partner moves in. But getting along with a gay parent's partner isn't necessarily any harder than getting along with a straight parent's new partner.

Children of gays must also deal with questions like, who can I tell? Will my friends think I'm gay because my mother/father's gay? Should I play it safe and laugh at the jokes told about gays at school, or should I take a big risk and say, "That's not funny"? But whatever the problems—and who doesn't have problems?—gay parents all around the country are successfully raising children right now.

Are there more gay people today than there used to be or are more just admitting they're gay?

There probably aren't any more today than there were in the past. But times have changed. Gays used to be in a closet so tightly shut it was suffocating. People were arrested for being actively gay, put in prison or in mental hospitals, fired from jobs. Much was done to make gays feel deeply guilty about their homosexuality. Gay Pride Day was unimaginable. Whatever the difficulties nowadays, it is much easier to be openly gay than it was a few decades ago. So gay people who would once have stayed in hiding have opened the closet door and stepped out.

What is outing?

When a gay man or lesbian openly acknowledges his or her sexual preference they are "out of the closet," or out. Often gays and lesbians are out only to a small circle of friends. In other cases they don't care who knows, or are eager and proud to acknowledge their sexual preference publicly. For entertainers, politicians, and other public figures coming out is a more complicated problem. While their sexual preference might be well known among their friends and co-workers, straight and gay, if they were known to be gay by the general public their careers might suffer. Everyone in Hollywood knew that Rock Hudson was gay, but it was only after he died of AIDS that this fact became generally known to the public, where he had once been regarded as a heterosexual sex symbol. Hiding like that has long irritated some of the more militant gay activists. One of their objections to famous people staying in the closet is that they believe young gays need prominent and successful people as positive role models. In the 1990s there has been a movement among some of the more radical gay activists, particularly the younger ones, to publicly identify prominent gays who don't want to be identified. The practice is known as "outing." Outing remains controversial in the gay community, and is often discussed and argued about.

Are people gay because the opposite sex finds them unattractive?

Are you kidding? Some of the world's most glamorous, famous, and beautiful people are gay. We can't tell you who they are because they could sue us. But we assure you there are gay movie stars, gay rock stars, and gay sports stars. There are also plenty of very good-looking gay people who aren't famous. Some spend a lot of their time firmly but

politely saying no to straight people who find them
very attractive indeed.

Do gay men hate women? Do lesbians hate men?

If gay men hate women, why do so many have
close female friends? And why do so many admire
legendary female stars like Judy Garland and Mari-
lyn Monroe? Rock star Madonna has a huge following among young gay guys.

No, if you want to talk about hatred, then let's talk
about how hatred is expressed. Rape, for example,
is an angry, violent, hating kind of crime. Women
are not raped by gay men. Wives are battered and
beaten by straight husbands. It's straight men who
buy the pornographic magazines that show women
bound and chained. Not gays.

Many lesbians are feminists who feel a strong
sense of kinship with straight women, probably
stronger than most gay men feel toward men who
are straight. They are perfectly comfortable leading
women-centered lives. This puzzles and even dis-
turbs those straight people who believe a woman's
life should always revolve around a man.

Man hating has nothing to do with the enjoyment
lesbians feel in each other's company, which ex-
tends far beyond sex. Lesbians play softball together, go on picnics together. Many have intense
long-term relationships. "We are women who love
women," lesbians say. Note that they do not describe themselves as "women who hate men."

Are there more gay males than lesbians?

Some experts say more males than females are gay, but who knows? Lesbians can hide more easily than gay men. Straight people aren't looking for them. And we're flexible about what's socially acceptable behavior in a woman, not so flexible when it comes to men.

When two women meet in public they can say hello with a hug and a kiss. Nobody minds. If two men greeted each other that way everybody on the street would become very nervous. If one woman is in jeans and the other wears a dress nobody pays any attention to them. People would definitely notice if one of the men was wearing a dress. If two women share an apartment for years nobody jumps to the conclusion they're gay. If two men shared an apartment for years—especially if they were even slightly effeminate—everybody would assume they were gay, even if they were straight.

Can you tell if someone is gay?

Gays are expected to fit a stereotype: The lisping male with limp wrists who calls everybody "Sweetie." The big, tough, mean-looking female who could punch out Mike Tyson. Yes, there are gay people who fit this image. There are straight people who fit this image, too, and who get hassled for looking "gay."

But there are a lot of gay people who don't fit the stereotype. There are tiny, delicate lesbians. There are huge, brawling gay male football players, masculine gay male Olympic gold medal winners, and

muscular gay male construction workers. Gays, like
straights, come in all shapes and sizes.

Interestingly, the stereotype of the effeminate
male has very little to do with femininity. When is
the last time a girl in your school bent her wrist,
flapped her hand, and lisped "Sweetie"? And what's
feminine about a male body in tight jeans? Yet when
a gay guy wears tight jeans straight people say he
looks like a girl.

How do gays find each other?

They meet at gay bars, through friends, at work,
or at parties. On college campuses they join gay organizations, which sponsor parties and dances. In
some big cities teens can meet at the gay community
center. In cities with large gay communities there
are many exclusively gay organizations such as a
gay men's chorus or a lesbian discussion group or
soccer team. The one place it's hard for gays to meet
is in the average high school. Schools often abandon gays, as principal, teachers, and students prefer
to pretend they do not exist.

Are there certain jobs gay people are mostly in?

Gays work everywhere. There are gay accoun-
tants, veterinarians, doctors, teachers, plumbers,
lawyers, scientists, architects, farmers, ranchers,
journalists, members of Congress, members of the
clergy, secretaries, models, computer programmers, waiters and waitresses, sales personnel, car
dealers, soldiers, sailors, tinkers, tailors . . . this
list could run forever. But when it comes to jobs
most gays—no matter how competent—are still in

the closet. Gays in search of freedom or gays who fit
the stereotype are often attracted to professions in
which they can be openly homosexual or where they
at least won't be hassled or physically attacked.

Straight women who would be upset to learn that
a policeman was gay don't mind having their hair
done by a gay male hairdresser. They've bought the
stereotype that policemen, since they're strong and
brave, just have to be straight. Hairdressers aren't
expected to go around arresting criminals. They can
be "sensitive." What this means is that the tough
gay policeman has to hide his homosexuality. The
gay hairdresser (sensitive or not) doesn't. No won-
der a lot of gay men become hairdressers.

Many years ago gays who weren't safe anywhere
else found a measure of freedom and acceptance in
the arts, which have always been a haven for rebels
and outsiders. Today you'll still find a high proportion of gays of both sexes in theater, music, film,
television, the visual arts, fashion, design, and writing.

While there is a high proportion of gays in the
entertainment world, many complain that they are
still presented unfairly, if at all, in films and on television. There are very few sympathetic gay characters on popular television shows. When one appears
the episode is immediately labeled as "controversial." Such shows are often confronted with threats
of boycott from conservative protesters and with the
withdrawal of some advertisers. While gays may be
"over represented" in the entertainment industry,
they are "under represented" in its product.

By and large lesbians do the same kind of work
other women do. Their incomes tend to be lower

than men's, but that holds for straight women, too. Lower income is one reason why lesbians are less visible than gay men. Gay men have the money to open bars and restaurants, to travel, and to set fashion trends. Lesbians don't.

One field lesbians are drawn to is sports, where they're not only athletes but coaches and phys ed teachers, too. They do face a lot of discrimination in sports-related jobs, though, if they're out of the closet. You'll find them in the military, too, though if discovered they can be kicked out. Some lesbians have sought jobs in traditionally male occupations. They've helped disprove the myth (once widely believed) that women can't be mechanics or builders, move heavy machinery, or drive trucks. Perhaps because they face so much discrimination gays of both sexes are drawn to humanitarian professions. There are gay therapists and social workers. You'll find gays working in hospitals. They are drawn to the ministry, and to education, too.

How do their families react to their being gay?

There are parents who are immediately understanding and supportive, but they're in the minority. Most parents need time. For some the first reaction is shock. Others pretend to themselves it can't be true. Some feel guilty and blame themselves. Others feel angry and blame their child. Some get so mad they kick their gay child out of the house.

Parents who thought their child would marry and have children of his or her own someday may mourn the grandchildren they'll never have. More worrisome than mere disappointment is the nagging fear of AIDS. (When it comes to AIDS lesbians have much less to fear than gay men. Lesbians are one of the lowest risk groups for AIDS in the country.) Parents of gays, and brothers and sisters of gays, too, ask themselves what their friends and relatives will think. Parents worry about gay bashing. Will their gay children be safe? Will they be lonely? Will they find jobs? Will being gay hurt their careers? Valid concerns!

The gay person's family probably knows very little about homosexuality. Most of what they've heard is wrong. But as time passes parents get over their initial shock. Gays learn they can confide in their brothers and sisters, often more easily than they can confide in their parents. The world doesn't come to an end when the neighbors find out. Parents learn their gay son practices safe sex. The whole family realizes that many of their original ideas about homosexuality were mistaken. They begin to form an honest relationship with the gay person, perhaps for the first time. They may all even wind up working together for gay rights.

How can you ask someone if they're gay without embarrassing them?

Adults may not find your question at all embarrassing. But it's not a good idea to ask teenagers flat out if they're gay unless they've tossed out clues that they want you to ask. They may not be fully out to themselves or they may be terrified that the news they're gay will get around school and they'll be teased, insulted, shunned, and even beaten up. If you show you're a good friend—understanding, tolerant, and able to keep a secret—he or she may very well tell you what you want to know without your asking. Gay teens often long for a sympathetic ear. But unless you're sure you're not just being nosy, let your friend choose the time and place. If the question slips out, don't press if the answer is no. Maybe your friend isn't ready to confide in anyone. Maybe your friend is straight.

Are gays promiscuous?

It's always been more socially acceptable for males to be promiscuous than females. Look around your school. You probably know some popular boy whose idea of a relationship is to pick up a girl, maybe have a pizza, go driving around, and then have sex. Nobody calls him a slut. But "slut" is still a label pinned on girls who are as quick to have sex. Yet the attitude that males get what they can and it's up to females to put on the brakes was once far more widespread than it is now.

It's an attitude that spilled over into the world of gay men. There was only one problem: There was no one to put on the brakes. The quick pickup, the bathhouse scene, and compulsive sex were a part of gay male life before AIDS. Promiscuity wasn't part of the life of all gay men. There were plenty of long-term, stable relationships. But there was lots of promiscuity as well. The young and good-looking were in demand. Others had to take what they could get. Many were very lonely.

There's another reason for the promiscuity. The quick pickup was often the only way gays could connect with each other at all. Police were always on the lookout for them, routinely raiding gay bars or entrapping them by pretending to be gay and then arresting them when they responded. Desperate and dangerous sexual encounters took place in parks, public bathrooms, and the backs of trucks. If caught, a gay man faced jail, public humiliation, loss of his job, the end of his marriage, and even violence. We know this sounds melodramatic, but that's how it was.

A heady freedom followed when the era of gay rights began. By then recreational sex had become a deeply ingrained gay male habit. AIDS changed all this. But for younger gays a change was in the wind anyway. They could meet in the open. They could take time to get to know each other. They could have relationships, not just encounters, and become partners as well as lovers.

What about women? In the days when the gay world was an underground world lesbians, too, had a very difficult time. Lonely, isolated, some grabbed sex and companionship when they could. But others managed to form surprisingly loving and stable relationships. And so did a lot of gay men. Not all gay males were promiscuous. Considering what gay people were up against back then, it's amazing there were any close long-term relationships at all.

To see how different it is today, check out your average college campus. You'll find there's an organization for gays. The organization sponsors parties and dances. Gay sex is fun for gays, and these dances and parties are not Sunday school outings. But neither are the parties going on at the fraternity houses on campus.

Is AIDS a punishment for being gay?

The idea that disease of any kind is a punishment unleashed on wicked and immoral people to ensure that they suffer for their sins is one that should go back where it belongs: to the twelfth century. It flies in the face of everything modern science has taught us. Though in the United States AIDS first appeared in the gay community, where it spread rapidly, it is not a "gay disease." Straight people can become infected with the AIDS virus, too. Gay males remain a high-risk group, but nowadays most practice safe sex. So should all sexually active straight teenagers. For more on this, read Chapter 8, which deals with AIDS.

Do gay men and lesbians get along well?

There are stresses and strains. After all, they are two distinct and separate groups. But they're strongly united on gay rights issues and they can count on one another in a crisis. When AIDS swept through the gay male community lesbians did everything they could to help. Today many lesbians are donating blood for AIDS patients.

Do gay men want to be women? Is that why they wear women's clothes and have sex-change operations?

Gay men do not want to be women and the vast majority do not wear women's clothes. But straight people have such a hard time believing this, and are so confused about the differences between drag queens, transvestites, and transsexuals, that it will take a whole chapter to clear things up. So take a look at Chapter 5. But get ready for some surprises.

3
All in the Family

"I come from a conservative Italian family, so conservative that when I first saw guys hugging and kissing each other in Greenwich Village even I thought they were weird. My brothers are straight and my father's always saying to me, 'You'll be the first to marry.' I think he's just trying to be an optimist because somewhere inside he really has an inkling that I'm gay." —ANTHONY V., AGE 17

"I told my mother I was gay driving home from Los Angeles at Christmas vacation and she said, 'It's about time you told me,' and proceeded to list all the boys I had ever gone out with." —JOHN L., AGE 18

Betty first learned her daughter was a lesbian in the principal's office when sixteen-year-old Kim broke down crying and confessed that she was gay. "I'd already suspected it, but it was like realizing your child is sick; when the doctor says your child is about to die, does it lessen the shock?"

Betty didn't know what to say to Kim. She was ashamed, angry, and blamed herself. This couldn't have happened if she had been a good mother. And what did the principal do while all this emotion swirled in the air? Nothing! He couldn't think of anything else to say so he told Betty to take Kim to their family doctor.

Of course, it isn't only parents of gays who have to face reality. You know yourself that straight teens often surprise, shock, even amaze their parents. Fathers who thought they'd get football players get violinists (and vice versa). Mothers who hoped for beauty pageant winners raise chubby daughters who like to read. The kid who always got A's in fifth grade upsets his parents by flunking French in tenth grade. But because most straight people know so little about homosexuality—and what they've heard is chiefly negative—finding out that a son or daughter is gay can make a parent feel as if a bomb has just exploded in the living room.

Who is this person they once thought they understood? Do they really know their child at all? To establish a good relationship with their gay son or daughter, parents have to say good-bye to the teenager they imagined they had, the one whose future they had mapped out. They've got to get to know and appreciate their child as he or she really is. For some parents the saying good-bye part of the process is tough, accompanied by the kind of grief, anger, and sadness usually experienced by people when they mourn the death of a loved one. For other parents the reaction is far less extreme. But rarely is coming out easy for parents of teens.

Parents may get mad. "Damn it, we've never had any 'faggots' in this family and we're not going to start now," or "I've put up with a lot from you but I'm not putting up with this." Others don't admit to themselves they've heard what they've heard. "Hm, that's interesting, but your aunt's coming over, Crissie. Would you drive to the 7-Eleven store and pick up some cookies?"

Some parents refuse to discuss it at all. "I don't want to hear about it, I don't want to know about it. It's your life, keep me out of it." Others say, "Teenagers go through a lot of phases, dear. This is just another one." And for many parents there's guilt. "Where did I go wrong?"

Betty lived in Texas all her life, but not in a big city like Houston or Dallas. "There's no large visible gay community anywhere near here, and if any of my friends or relatives are gay they haven't told me. Before Kim came out to me last year I had never read about homosexuality. I had no knowledge of it. I didn't know where to turn. I didn't know what to do. Last year was like living in a battle zone."

How had Kim and Betty wound up in the principal's office? "I overheard a phone conversation of Kim's, not about homosexuality, but about her being called into his office. When she caught me listening she changed the subject, but she didn't fool me. I knew she was in some kind of trouble. Her grades were falling. Something was bothering her. So I went to see the principal."

The principal told Betty that Kim had been skipping classes and called Kim into his office. He asked her what was wrong. Betty asked her what was wrong. Their voices grew louder, their questions more persistent. Under all this pressure Kim broke down.

"The reason I'd already suspected my daughter was a lesbian—even though I wouldn't let myself believe it—is because she's blond and pretty and boys are very attracted to her. Yet she treated them as if they would violate her and she was very protective of her girlfriends. She's an aggressive basketball player, the star of the girls' team, and the only people she knew well were the girls on the team. Later I learned that she hadn't had any sexual experiences with girls at the time of the incident in the principal's office, but at fifteen she'd fallen in love with a straight girl on the team. It was very painful for Kim because she couldn't come out to the girl, to me, to anyone. Poor kid. At least she was out to herself.''

What happened next is typical. Betty took Kim to a psychiatrist. "The psychiatrist didn't know much about homosexuality. He blamed my husband and me for it. That only made things worse. I was convinced Kim could change if she loved me enough. We took her to another psychiatrist, one who agreed with me she could change. Kim quit therapy. Now I know how important it is to find a therapist who's not anti-gay. But back then I didn't know anything and I was going crazy. I was such a wreck my husband was more worried about me than he was about Kim.''

The distance between Kim and her mother grew wider. There were fights, tears, periods of sullen silence. Finally Kim became so unhappy Betty was afraid she might run away or try to commit suicide. "I realized I couldn't go on rejecting Kim. I had to force myself to accept her lesbianism somehow. But how?''

She began by looking for books on homosexuality in the local library. "I was looking for books for

Kim as well as for myself. Kim would rather have died than take out a book about being gay herself. I didn't find anything helpful."

Next Betty, who is Catholic, turned to her church. "I got no help. Then I phoned the hospitals. I met a blank wall. But even though I didn't seem to be getting anywhere, inside I was changing. I was getting closer to Kim. It wasn't me against her anymore. It was us against the world together."

Betty went on the offensive. "I complained to my priest. I said, 'A gay teenager should be told he or she is a child of God.' I fought with the high school principal. I told him he should have done more than send us to our family doctor. Why isn't there anything in the school for gays? They've got school programs for everyone else. There's even help for drug addicts. The gay kid is stuck there in school with nothing, goes to the principal and all the principal can say is 'Go home and tell your parents!' He should know the last thing a teenager can do is go home and tell his parents when he's afraid his parents will reject him, maybe even throw him out. Well, Kim's a senior now with only a few months left in that school. I'll be glad when she's out of there. I still don't know very much about homosexuality but I know I love my daughter. I don't want to lose Kim."

Will, eighteen, a freshman at Harvard, lives in an affluent New England community. His father is a doctor, his mother a lawyer. Will has three older brothers who are straight. Will is gay. Let's hear from his father.

"When Will suggested we take a long walk together on the beach one Saturday afternoon I could tell he wanted to talk about something. He started telling me about a friend who was gay. It was a roundabout way of telling me he was gay. He dropped several hints about himself and I turned and hugged him and said, 'It's fine, Will. It doesn't make any difference.' But on the drive home I began to worry. When we got home I told my wife, Carrie. She was hurt because Will told me, not her. Then she kept asking me, was I sure it was true? Did he really say he was gay? I said yes, it's true. So she wrote him a letter telling him how much she loved him and he phoned us as soon as he got it."

Will had already come out to his brothers. "They accepted his homosexuality instantly. It took Carrie and me longer. Now we've told the whole family except for Carrie's father, who is very old and very conservative. Will has changed us. We're more open-minded now, more tolerant than we used to be. And not just about homosexuality. We're proud of Will. He's an excellent student. He brought his boyfriend home over Thanksgiving vacation and Carrie and I like him very much. You see, it isn't enough that a parent accept his gay child. To be fully a part of his life you have to accept his life-style and care about the people he cares about."

There are parents who like to wear their children as ornaments. They want children who make them look good. Peggy, whose daughter Carol is a lesbian, says, "I'm all frills and laces. My husband's very masculine. He used to drive race cars when he was younger. We're the all-American couple, picture perfect. Or at least we were until my youngest daughter, Carol, was born. My oldest daughter is typically girly-girly, but Carol was always a tomboy. She liked to dress up as Superman on Halloween when she was only four years old. Carol was an active, cheerful child, but in junior high she changed. She began having severe headaches. I think it was because she was trying to deal with her sexual feelings.

"It didn't help that we live in a nice cozy suburb. There's a superficial kind of caring where we live, but no blacks are here, no minorities, of any kind, everybody's the same. Our neighbors don't really tolerate difference or dissent. I'm out about Carol to only one neighbor and a few personal friends. And there's a lot of one-upmanship, a lot of competition. Who has the most money? Who has the most successful children? Where we live homosexuality is certainly not considered a sign of success.

"I didn't realize Carol was gay at first, because she went out with boys. Gay kids sometimes think they're bisexual at first. Maybe Carol did, too. She had a boyfriend at the same time she had her first gay relationship. She was sixteen. But I began to notice things. Her relationship with her girlfriend was much more intense than her relationship with her boyfriend. The girl slept over all the time and there was lots of fighting and jealousy. I resisted seeing what was going on. Carol gave me hints but I refused to admit to her that I'd picked them up. I did what a lot of parents do in a similar situation: I made anti-gay remarks (they were my hints) to test her reaction, but Carol refused to respond. This little game went on for about a year.

"Finally I had to accept what I was seeing, but I

told myself that since Carol went out with boys as well as girls sooner or later she'd turn exclusively to boys. But it turned out the other way round. She came out to me just before she graduated from high school. She told me she'd dated boys because other girls did and that she'd had sexual relationships with boys. The sex was okay but there was a feeling of emptiness. She could only love a girl. Carol was afraid to tell her father, but when she did he handled it well. I'm not sure he'd be so accepting if he had a son who was gay."

If straight parents have gay kids, there are also straight kids with gay parents. As one gay father told us, "For a gay parent, coming out to your kids is like jumping into the unknown, falling off a tightrope. How will your children react? It's hard to be honest. It takes some parents years to tell their kids. Look, kids have things they fear to discuss with their parents. Well, the same emotions and risks are there for parents when the parents are gay.

"It's easier to tell children before the teen years. I know one father who told his daughter when she was small, and they've got a wonderful relationship. She's in her early teens now and he takes her to malls where they check out the boys together playfully while they go shopping. They kid around a lot about which guys are cute. If a teenager thinks a parent is gay the teenager should bring the subject up. Calm and quiet works best. If the teenager sounds hostile the parent will just retreat.

"Wives often have trouble accepting a husband's homosexuality. My wife tried to be understanding, but no matter how well wives react at first they usually become angry later, when husbands leave them for male lovers. If the wife is very hostile and belligerent the kids will often side with the father. They come to see him as a rebellious hero who shares problems with them.

"It's harder for a father to come out to a teenage son than to a teenage daughter. When I separated from my wife my youngest son was sixteen. The two older children, both girls, responded well, but my son was shocked. He became jealous of my lover, claiming I was spending too much time with him. But I don't think that would have been any different if my lover had been a woman."

Jason, who's straight and just finishing his first year of college, has known that his mother is a lesbian since he was two. "I'm close to my mother, though I lived with my father when I was in high school. It took some of the pressure off. My mother's a strong woman who won't compromise her principles. She's out to the world. So before I introduce people to her I always tell them she's a lesbian since they will definitely pick it up."

What Jason found hardest to take in high school were jokes about gays. They weren't directed against him but they hurt. "My mother's white and my father's black and I would have stood up to anybody who made a racial joke because racial issues are out in the open. Gay issues aren't. I didn't know any openly gay teens at school and most of the time I went along with the jokes. In high school you just try to save yourself."

When someone in a family is gay, in a sense the whole family's in the closet. Who do they tell? Jason is out to his girlfriend about his mother. She was upset at first, but "I wouldn't go out with a girl long if she wasn't open-minded enough to accept my mother."

Jason's advice to teenagers who suddenly learn a parent is gay? "Don't feel betrayed. Try to understand why your parent kept this from you for so long. Gay people don't feel safe. Maybe your parent was trying to protect you from being persecuted, embarrassed, or hurt. Try to talk to your parents about this without screaming or shouting.

"But no matter what the problems, it's good that you know because otherwise you may misread what's going on in your parents' lives. Gays in the closet can be very unhappy, which affects the people they live with. They may seem very hostile and their children won't know why. The other parent doesn't know what's wrong either, so things can be a real mess and nobody can make things better because of the secrecy."

Noelle, sixteen, is a cheerleader who lives with her mother. Her parents are divorced. Her father, an art teacher, isn't out at work because he's afraid he'll lose his job. Noelle, who's very popular, is afraid to tell anyone at school. "I wish I could talk to the kids who have the wrong ideas about gays, who call them 'queers.' I wish I could tell them what my father's like. I wish I knew other kids who have gay parents. All I can do is 'talk' to my diary."

Diane is a lesbian whose three sons live with her. Matt, thirteen, hasn't told the kids at school about his mother, but "I tell them to shut up when they make 'faggot' jokes." Stuart, fifteen, has more conflicts. "I don't talk about my mother's being gay with my friends because then my friends might think I'm gay. I tell people the woman who lives with us—Anita, my mother's partner—is her cousin."

Adam, sixteen, won't talk about homosexuality at school, either. "Someone might say something that would make me mad. Except for liking their own sex, gay people are just like straight people—only straight kids don't know it."

"Kids develop a sixth sense about who to tell and who not to tell," says Diane. "I leave my gay books on the shelves when kids come to stay over, which they do very often, and they don't notice. But I am careful to wear feminine clothes when I go to the boys' school. People see what they want to see, and if you're a woman who doesn't look like the stereotype of a 'bull dyke' kids just assume you're straight. My sons make up whatever they think fits to protect themselves. They thought up the cousin stuff for Anita. I've advised the boys to be very careful who they come out to about me at school, especially the girls they fall in love with who might spread the word around. I know a teenager just coming out who filled her notebook with thoughts about a girl she has a crush on and someone in class found it and told everyone. It was horrible.

"Lesbians usually hide in school—it's easier to play the game than put up with the hassles. And there's so little information. You don't see much about lesbians in movies or on television. When the media focuses on homosexuality it's usually gay men. I had no idea I was gay when I was growing up. I didn't know a word for what I felt, but I was always more aware of women than men. Not that an occasional fantasy or crush or even a gay affair means you're gay. Only when it's a consistent, constant, satisfying way of life are you gay. I ran away from it. I even got married. But I finally accepted it. Do you know, some of my relatives still won't speak to me."

Justine is a senior in high school. Her parents are divorced. She has chosen to live with her father, who's gay. He isn't out to her mother. He isn't out to her sister. Nor is he out at work. But he trusts Justine. He came out to her when she was sixteen. Justine agreed not to tell her mother, who would be hurt and who might blame all the problems in the marriage on her husband's homosexuality, "which just isn't true. I love my father. He's been wonderful to me. He's always had a great sense of humor. I have pictures of him crawling around with me when I was a baby. He's fun. He'll tease and say, 'Hey, I'm a fruit' in front of me and my grandparents and everyone laughs. He raised me not to be prejudiced against anybody and he's always supported my choice of boyfriends, so I feel I should be supportive of him, too."

Justine hasn't told her friends or her boyfriend about her father. "I would if our relationship ever became serious. I couldn't marry someone who didn't accept my father. But it's hard to talk to my friends. They're all so sure homosexuality is wrong. I try to defend gays in a general way without getting personal. My friends think they can always spot a gay person when they see one, which makes me laugh because they never suspect my father."

What about friendships between straight people and gay people? Can they work? Jon and Amanda, both eighteen, say yes. Best friends since sixth grade, they graduated from high school together last June and share an apartment. They have part-time jobs and go to a community college located in the small city where they live.

Jon is gay. Amanda's straight. Here's what she says. "Straight friends often ask me how I can stand the kissing and hugging that goes on right in front of me when Jon's boyfriend comes over. I tell them it's no problem. They're just expressing affection. My boyfriend, Craig, doesn't feel comfortable with Jon, either. Craig goes to the same school I do but he lives with his parents because it's cheaper. Craig used to worry that Jon would want to have a sexual relationship with me. When he realized Jon didn't want to make love to me and I didn't want to make love to Jon he still felt uncomfortable. It embarrasses him that I'm living with a gay person. People tease him about it. He hates to come over when Jon's gay friends are around.

"I get tired of everyone asking me, 'Why do you live with someone gay?' They forget Jon is an old friend. They look at him and they see a gay person. I look at him and I see Jon. My mother's an alcoholic and I told Jon about her in seventh grade when I couldn't talk about her drinking with anyone else. He was very understanding, maybe because he sensed he was gay. We were both people with secrets we couldn't shout to the world."

But if Amanda shared her secret with Jon in seventh grade, Jon didn't come out to Amanda until senior year. By then Jon had come out to other people—people whose friendship he was willing to lose if they couldn't accept his homosexuality. But risk losing Amanda's friendship? That was different.

"Jon and I were in a restaurant when he gave me a message written in the code we'd made up in sixth grade. He told me not to decipher the message until I got home, and then he went off to the bathroom. He knew I'd read the note. He just didn't want to be there facing me when I learned he was gay."

But Amanda didn't say anything to Jon when he came back. She needed time. She went home and thought things through. Next day in school she told Jon it didn't make any difference. What made a difference was that he hadn't told her sooner.

"He said he didn't think I was ready to hear it before. He may be right. Up to my senior year I probably would have worried about what my friends would think. Then there's AIDS. Jon is very careful, but would that have meant anything to me a couple of years ago? I don't know."

And now? "My friends know if they made me choose between Jon and them I'd choose Jon."

4 One in Ten

I've always liked the look of women's hands and felt it would be nicer to be touched by a woman's hands than a man's."

—SHEILA G., AGE 15

"When other kids were having fun it was empty for me. When you're out with a girl what do you do? My mind went back to the locker room and what other boys say you do. Even half nude I said to myself, 'What do I do?' I had no doubt about what to do when I was first with a boy." —KYLE D., AGE 18

In the 1940s and early 1950s a biologist named Alfred C. Kinsey, who had spent most of his career studying tiny wasps, undertook a massive study of the sexual behavior of American males and females. Kinsey and his associates carried out in-depth interviews with thousands of Americans. The results of the study hit the nation like a bombshell. Kinsey was denounced as a liar, a subversive, a pervert, a threat to morality and the American family, etc. Attempts were made to ban the Kinsey reports from the mails as "pornography." Politicians were partially successful at having funds for further research by Kinsey cut off. Alternate funds were found, but it took time and trouble.

What so outraged many people (and fascinated many others) was Kinsey's conclusion that a lot of people didn't lead the sort of sex lives that law, custom, and public morality said they should. Actually, most people who lived in the 1950s knew very well that a lot of people said one thing about sex and did another. But to have it come out publicly, in a scientific study, that was the shock. There was a lot of premarital sex and extramarital sex reported, and that came as no big surprise, but there was also a lot of homosexuality reported. That was a surprise. Even the Kinsey researchers were surprised. Over the years Kinsey and the institute that he founded have concluded that about 13 percent of adult males and 7 percent of adult females are exclusively or predominately homosexual for significant periods of their lives. That averages out to about 10 percent of the total adult population. A far, far larger percentage has had some kind of homosexual experience at some point in their lives.

What Kinsey's studies showed, and what an awful lot of people did not want to accept and still don't want to accept, is the fact that homosexuality was not some sort of exotic sin or rare deviation from the norm, but a fairly common part of human sexual behavior.

Kinsey had made a career of taxonomy—the classification of living things. Experience had taught him that there were no sharp boundaries or convenient classifications in nature. He carried this view to the study of human sexuality. Of male homosexuality, he wrote:

"Males do not represent two discrete populations, heterosexual and homosexual. The world is not to be divided into sheep and goats. Not all things are black nor all things white. It is a fundamental of taxonomy that nature rarely deals with discrete categories. Only the human mind invents categories and tries to force facts into separate pigeon-holes. The living world is a continuum in each and every one of its aspects. The sooner we learn this concerning human sexual behavior the sooner we shall reach a sound understanding of the realities of sex."

Back in the 1950s when Kinsey made that statement it seemed an outrageous and immoral one to lots of people. Many would still regard such a view as outrageous and immoral. Yet Alfred Kinsey was a fine scientist. He applied the scientific method, as best he could, to the difficult and extremely sensitive area of human behavior.

Sex and science have always been an explosive combination.

In this chapter we are first going to take a look at what science has discovered about homosexuality. And then we are going to look at how, if at all, these findings have been used. A word or two of warning here. When we use phrases like "what science has discovered," that sounds very authoritative, very final. In fact, science rarely provides complete and final answers to questions. Any scientific conclusion can be overturned by new facts and new interpretations. It happens all the time. This is particularly true in the area of human sexual behavior. Various experts and authorities looking at the same information often come to very different conclusions. Practically everything is controversial. We will try to present the best information available, information on which there is substantial agreement; but we acknowledge that there will always be some disagreement.

Something else to keep in mind is that science tries to describe and understand what is, in this case how people really behave, and why; not how we think they should behave. As Kinsey found out, a lot of people don't like the information that science turns up. They try to deny it, or say that somehow this knowledge is dangerous and harmful. For example, some have complained that because Kinsey and others found that homosexuality is common, that information will "promote" homosexual behavior. That's just the opposite of what the facts show. The Kinsey report didn't create a large number of homosexuals—they were already there before the report was ever issued. Suppressing this information, or denying it, wouldn't make the homosexuals disappear.

Two hundred years ago the subject of homosexuality was almost completely the domain of religion. It was sin and that was that. In the nineteenth century there was a gradual shift in emphasis from the religious to the medical. Homosexuality came to be regarded as more of an illness or mental disorder than an actual sin. It was something to be treated by the physician as well as the priest. The aura of immorality remained. If it was a disease, it was supposed to be a shameful one. The problem was that the physicians didn't understand homosexuality, and they certainly couldn't cure it. They searched for causes, investigating everything from genital abnormalities to hormone imbalances, but could find nothing physical that distinguished the homosexual from the heterosexual. Treatments involved everything from cold baths and hypnosis to conditioning and painful electroshock. Treatments for any sort of "sexual disorder" could be pretty brutal. In the early nineteenth century American children who masturbated were sometimes tied to their beds, and for "hopeless cases" a few physicians actually recommended castration! It was supposed to be better than the moral degradation and eventual insanity masturbation was supposed to bring. Really, people believed this!

Psychotherapy, which began to take hold in America during the 1930s and 1940s, was more humane. It involved long sessions in which the patient simply talked to the therapist. The aim was to uncover the childhood events that had created the patient's problems, such as homosexuality. The theory then was that the cause of homosexuality in men was a family with a strong and domineering mother and a weak or absent father. Most homosexuals over the age of forty who came from relatively affluent backgrounds recall years of expensive sessions of therapy aimed at curing, or changing, their sexual orientation. The therapy may have helped them in a variety of ways, but it rarely "cured" their homosexuality. Often it made them feel worse.

Moreover, psychologists and psychiatrists were encountering homosexuals who, aside from their sexual preferences, seemed quite normal and well adjusted in other ways. Whatever troubles they might have had did not stem so much from their homosexuality as from the way society treated them, and from being told that they were sick and degenerate people.

Information from other branches of science was filling out the picture. Anthropologists found that homosexuals existed in practically every society they studied. In some societies, many American Indian tribes, for example, homosexuality was regarded as quite natural. In other societies it was hidden or forbidden. But open or hidden, it was almost always there. Information about homosexual activity in some societies was considered so shocking that it was often played down or left out, even in scientific reports. But eventually it came to light.

One of the requirements of science is that basic assumptions be constantly questioned, reexamined. If they no longer fit the available facts, then the basic assumptions should be changed. One of those changes took place in 1967, when the American Psychiatric Association officially removed homosexuality from its list of mental disorders. The move was not without controversy. A vote on the issue found that a substantial minority, some 37 percent of the organization's members, wanted to keep homosexuality on the list of disorders. There are still psychiatrists who consider homosexuality a mental disorder. But it was off the APA's list, and it has stayed off. There are still psychiatrists and others who try to "cure" or "change" homosexual orientation. But there is no evidence that such treatments work. And there are fewer and fewer reputable therapists who even make the attempt.

By the way, a lot of scientists don't like the term

homosexuality at all. In 1978 the Kinsey Institute issued a massive study on the subject that was called *Homosexualities*. The report found that the subjects had a wide variety of life-styles, ranging from long-term, monogamous, marriage-type relationships to infrequent, furtive, and usually guilt-plagued sex. However, the overwhelming impression left by this report was of the sheer ordinariness of the lives of most gay people. The report's conclusion was that, aside from sexual orientation, homosexuals are not very different from mainstream Americans.

The cause of homosexuality has also been a matter of great controversy. Early in this century the cause of homosexuality was thought to be some sort of physical or mental disease or simply "moral weakness." Later, emphasis shifted to the environmental—a family in which a dominant, overprotective mother and weak father created a son's homosexuality. No single popular theory emerged as to the cause of lesbianism, and lesbians by and large have received much less attention from psychiatrists and sex researchers than have male homosexuals.

In 1983, Drs. Lee Ellis and Ashley Ames sat down to review all of the relevant studies on the origins of sexual orientation that had been done over the previous twenty-five years or so. Their review was to include animal studies, as well as studies of human development and behavior. The doctors thought the task would take a couple of months, and the work could be summarized in about twenty pages. Instead it took over three years, and the paper was nearly a hundred pages long.

The conclusion that they came to, after reviewing all the work that had been done, was that sexual orientation is largely determined by a "complex combination of genetic, hormonal, neurological, and environmental factors operating prior to birth. . . . In human beings, sexual orientation is determined between the second and fifth months of pregnancy. Sexual orientation is not learned, is not changed by the parents' personalities, and is not to be changed."

In short, most homosexuals were born with the tendency to be homosexual: They didn't choose it, and it can't easily be changed. Ellis and Ames concluded, "Theoretically, changing a homosexual's orientation should be just as difficult and as emotionally wrenching as changing a heterosexual's orientation."

In 1986, Dr. Richard Green, professor of psychiatry at the University of California at Los Angeles, published a long-term study of extremely effeminate boys. The boys had first been examined in early childhood and had been tracked into adolescence and young adulthood. The majority, three-fourths, matured into homosexuals or bisexuals. Sensitive parents and professional counseling might make the boys more well adjusted and happier, but did not seem to change their basic sexual orientation.

Dr. Judd Marmor, a past president of the American Psychiatric Association, called this study "most important."

"Society tends to treat male homosexuals as if they had a choice about their sexual orientation, when in fact they have no more choice about how they develop than heterosexuals do," he said.

Dr. Allan Bell, a director of the Kinsey Institute, said that the findings didn't surprise him at all, because they corresponded to the data the Institute had been collecting for years.

In 1991 Dr. Simon LeVay, a neurobiologist at the Salk Institute in La Jolla, California, announced that he had found that the brains of homosexual men are structurally different from those of heterosexual men in a region thought to influence male sexual behavior.

If the discovery was confirmed it would be the first detection of a distinct pattern in the brain that could help explain sexual preference among men. Dr. LeVay found that one segment of the hypothalamus, an important structure in the brain, is only a quarter to a half the size in homosexual men than it is in heterosexual men. For homosexual men this area is more like that found in the brains of heterosexual women. The size difference was dramatic and it was the sort of difference that the public could easily grasp and understand.

The key phrase, however, is "if the discovery was confirmed." The announcement got an enormous amount of attention. It was on the front page of *The New York Times* and on all the network TV news shows. It was the subject of many talk shows. Predictably, those who insist that homosexuality results from a bad moral choice rather than being an inborn biological imperative disputed the finding.

In fact, there are many reasons to be cautious about the study, as even Dr. LeVay and his supporters point out. It was a tiny study using samples from the autopsied brain tissue of 19 homosexual men, 16 presumed heterosexual men, and six women also presumed to be heterosexual. All the homosexual men died of AIDS. It is only since the AIDS epidemic that medical researchers have been able to identify homosexual and heterosexual men. Before AIDS, sexual preference was rarely mentioned in medical records.

In medical research a lot of promising early studies do not live up to their expectations. Usually a preliminary study like this would never have received much attention beyond that of a very small group of researchers. It is almost unprecedented for basic biological research to generate this much interest. But the question of why an individual is a homosexual is such a hotly disputed topic in our society that this interesting, but far from conclusive, finding was front-page news.

Let's stop for a moment. By now some of you are worrying about that time when you were twelve and were "experimenting" with sex. Or when you were thirteen and had a "crush" on someone of the same sex. You're thinking, "Does this mean I'm homosexual and there's nothing I can do about it?" Not at all.

Remember what Kinsey said about the world not being divided into nice neat categories. We have said repeatedly, and will say again, that a large percentage of the population has had homosexual experiences or homosexual feelings—often during childhood or adolescence. Most do not become homosexual. It is for the majority a phase that ends naturally and usually without any special counseling or treatment. But for the minority—about 10 percent of the total population—it's no phase. They are homosexual.

The idea that there can be—that there are—homosexual teenagers still upsets a lot of people. Many, including doctors and others who really should know better, try to deny or ignore the mass of information that has been collected since the first Kinsey studies in 1948. They still prefer to regard homosexuality as something that appears, more or less spontaneously, in adults. Often it is said to be the result of a moral "choice" or a bad family environment, or of some sort of traumatic experience, like being "seduced" by an older homosexual. But the facts just don't support any of these ideas.

Most people like to think of children and adolescents as basically "innocent" and "good." It's very upsetting to face up to the fact that some of these children and adolescents are also gay or lesbian—which most people consider "bad" or "sick." It's far more comfortable to ignore the facts and pretend that teenage homosexuals don't exist, or that they are such a tiny and deranged minority that they are not worth bothering about.

In 1986, Dr. Gary Remafedi wrote an article on "Homosexual Youth" for the *Journal of the American Medical Association*, one of the most important medical journals in the world. He pointed out that despite the mountain of evidence a lot of authorities still rejected the idea that homosexual orientation can be established early in life. This rejection, he noted, was more than an abstract argument over the interpretation of statistics; by not recognizing the existence of teenage homosexuals, "it potentially damages the lives of millions of persons."

Dr. Remafedi wrote about the hostile attitudes of many doctors toward homosexuals. He cited a survey of doctors in which fully one-third said that their dislike of homosexuals would probably affect the way they treated homosexual patients. In the same survey, three-fourths of the doctors believed that their colleagues also disliked homosexuals and would probably treat them differently.

Dr. Remafedi went on to say, "Negative biases are also commonly espoused by other critical persons in the adolescent's milieu, including school principals, teachers, coaches, counselors, and peers"—that's you.

Being a teenager is tough enough. Being a homosexual teen is much tougher, and more dangerous, for a variety of reasons.

A 1988 study by the federal government concluded that homosexual teens face an enormous number of problems—physical, psychological, and social—and that not enough was being done for them. However, the findings of the study were not made public. Gay groups claimed that the study was suppressed by the conservative Reagan administration because many in the administration didn't like the conclusion that there were a lot of homosexual teens who were being badly treated and needed help. The findings of the study leaked out anyway.

First there is the threat of AIDS. That is a subject that we'll look at more fully in Chapter 8. But there are lots of other problems.

A gay or lesbian teen grows up in a world that still refuses to recognize that he or she exists. When the gay or lesbian teen's existence is recognized, the reaction is usually a bad one. He or she is said to be sinful, sick, disobedient, self-destructive, or just plain weak. He or she may be disowned by family

and friends, be verbally and physically abused, and
be told that the only solution is to change what can't
be changed. The abuse problem is not a small one.
One study found that 30 percent of gay male teens
were victims of physical assault, and many of the
assaults took place on school property. Over half of
the teens reported regular verbal abuse from class-
mates.

Where can the gay or lesbian teen turn for understanding and help? As Dr. Remafedi points out,
many of the traditional helpers—doctors, counselors, even teachers—are not available.

Suicide is a large and apparently growing problem among teens. Some studies indicate that teenage suicide rates have jumped, incredibly, over 300
percent in the past twenty years. Suicide is now one
of the leading causes of death among young people.
There are no firm statistics, but a host of reports
indicate that the rate of attempted and completed
suicide is far higher among gay and lesbian teens
than among the general teenage population. Drug
and alcohol abuse, serious depression, running
away from home, and dropping out of school may
also be more common for young gays and lesbians.

Is this another sign that gays and lesbians are basically sick and self-destructive individuals? That argument has been made. But it seems to us far more
reasonable to conclude that it's not so much same-
sex attraction as the way everyone else reacts to it
that drives many teens to and beyond the brink of
suicide.

Unfortunately, not enough people seem to care.
Dr. Remafedi points out that despite the indications
that homosexual adolescents appear to be at high

risk for suicide, the subject simply has not been studied.

Dr. Remafedi concludes that most homosexual teens are not getting "appropriate health care services and support from family and community" and therefore "are in jeopardy of serious emotional, social, and physical difficulties."

What about school? Has the subject of homosexuality ever been discussed in any of your classes? If so, try to remember what was said. Very little, we would suspect. Attempts at in-depth discussion of homosexuality in the classroom are often denounced as immoral or as somehow "promoting homosexuality." As if going to class will make you gay! Any teacher who proposes a study of homosexuality will immediately find himself or herself under suspicion of being "one of them." And in some places being "one of them" could get a teacher fired. A recent Gallup survey found that more than half of the population thought gays and lesbians should not be allowed to work in schools. There are almost certainly gay or lesbian teachers in your school. Are any of them open? And, by the way, what's the attitude of the other kids toward those who are simply suspected of being "queer"? Has a coach in your school ever been disciplined by the school administration for calling a losing team "a bunch of faggots"? Has anyone in your school ever been called on the carpet for telling "fag jokes"? What would happen if a guidance counselor in your school advised a homosexual student to contact one of the many gay or lesbian aid groups? Would the counselor be congratulated or fired? And finally, what would happen if a group of gays and lesbians in your school tried to set up their own group or club? Would the school administration recognize such a group and give them a room to meet in? What would the reaction of the other students be? What would *your* reaction be?

The Harvey Milk School, which opened in New York City in 1985, exemplifies the difficulties faced by a school system that tries to deal humanely and effectively with gay and lesbian teens. Harvey Milk was a popular and openly gay city supervisor in San Francisco who was murdered and is regarded as a hero and martyr in the gay community. The Harvey Milk School wasn't so much a "gay school" as a small alternative education program. Those who enrolled in the school were individuals who had already been beaten up or harassed and had dropped out or been driven out of their regular schools. They were going nowhere. The aim of the program was to help these kids catch up on their studies, deal with their problems, and get them back into a traditional school. If that proved impossible they could continue their studies at the Harvey Milk School and get a diploma.

It was a program, like many others, to help troubled kids finish school. And it was a very small one, involving just a handful of kids. Yet when news of the existence of the Harvey Milk School hit the press, there were howls of outrage, from politicians, religious groups, and others, that the New York City schools were "promoting homosexuality." Let us remind you that those who went to the school were already openly homosexual and had no other place to turn. Without the program they would be on the streets.

Fortunately, the New York City school system didn't back down, and the program continued and continues to this day. New York has a large and politically active gay community that was able to mount a counteroffensive. But that gives you an idea of just how difficult it is to make any attempt, no matter how modest and well intentioned, to help gay and lesbian teens.

The news isn't all grim. There is at the very least a growing awareness that homosexual teens *exist*. And all but the most hysterical and moralistic will admit that they have special problems and needs during the always turbulent teenage years.

It's a start. There is still a long, long way to go.

5
Drag Queens, Transvestites, and Transsexuals

Back in Chapter 2 we gave a brief answer to a question about whether homosexuals liked to dress up like the other sex or actually wanted to become the other sex. We said that the answer to that question was a lot more complicated and a lot more surprising than you might imagine, and that we would take the subject up again when we could expand on it. That time has now come. We are going to introduce you to three people that you would probably not meet at the local shopping mall—or if you did meet them, you wouldn't know who they were.

GLENDA Meet Glenda Starr. Glenda is tall, graceful, and glamorous. Glenda has long dark hair. An ankle bracelet winks from one smooth, nylon-encased slim leg. Glenda's dress is silky. Around Glenda's shoulders a bright scarf sparkles with glitter. Glenda is flirtatious, charming, and utterly feminine. Who is Glenda Starr? She's the personal creation of an eighteen-year-old gay female impersonator ("drag queen") named Gavin.

When the macho guys in your school cross-dress (dress in clothing appropriate to the opposite sex) on Halloween or talent night in the auditorium, they stuff pillows in their sweaters. They sway their hips wildly when they walk. They totter on high-heeled shoes. It's a joke.

There's nothing brash, silly, or exaggerated about Glenda. So subtle is Gavin's impersonation that he attended a senior prom as Glenda and no one—male or female—guessed he was really a boy. Gavin's date was gay. Both boys enjoyed breaking the rule that says you take a person of the opposite sex to your prom—whether you're straight or gay.

Let Gavin tell you. "The prom invitation said C.C. and date: Glenda Starr. It was fantastic. One thing surprised me, though. I never knew girls went into the washroom together. Boys always go alone. So I went to the ladies' room alone. It was full of girls talking about their dates. I loved listening to their conversations."

It's experiences like this, filled with risk and even danger, that help explain why Gavin finds cross-dressing exhilarating. "Drag is a year-round Halloween. You really go to extremes."

Fooling people isn't easy, and to become Glenda Gavin has to go through a long, arduous process. "When I went out with girls (I used to be in the closet) I always wondered why it took my dates so long to put on makeup. Now I know."

For Gavin makeup is only the beginning. By the time he's put on the chest, the wig, the foam rubber that goes around his hips, he's undergone a profound change, and it's not just physical. "I become a different person. My whole attitude changes. I'm much more confident as Glenda than as Gavin. That's the way it goes with drag. I have a friend who's modest and gentle who becomes wild and aggressive, even violent, when he's in drag."

Would Gavin like to be a girl if he could? No. If he were a girl he'd be an ordinary-everyday-version-of-Gavin kind of female. No physical transformation could ever turn him into Glenda for real. She's a role he plays, an imaginary character he's invented. "A drag queen is an actor one hundred percent."

But few actors identify so fully with their characters. By breaking the dress code (for example, wearing a bra and nylons, something he'd never dream of doing as Gavin) he breaks other barriers as well, including inner ones. He becomes a fascinating, intriguing, exciting person. Glenda is a star. She shines. She wins. "If I [Gavin] made a mistake, like falling down on the dance floor, everybody'd laugh. If Glenda fell down she'd handle it beautifully. She'd triumph! No one would laugh at her."

Why does Gavin see glamour and charisma as purely feminine traits? He isn't sure himself. All he knows is he does. So do the other female impersonators he knows. One friend so admires a famous fashion model that he follows her career by buying all the fashion magazines to see her pictures.

Gavin loves attention. "There's a lot of curiosity about drag queens. This is going to be the most popular chapter in your book. Drag is fun. Straight people go to drag shows. A female impersonator is an entertainer." And entertain he does. On weekends

Gavin, who began as a dancer, performs in drag in clubs around New York City. He sometimes thinks about becoming a stage or film actor, but he knows Glenda is his best act, the one special role he plays to perfection.

The rest of the time he's happy being Gavin. It's as Gavin, bright and articulate, that he attends classes at college. It's primarily as Gavin that he goes out on dates. And sex? He likes the shape of his body. He likes gay sex. He likes being male. He's out to his family. "It was very difficult. I had to come out to them twice, first as gay and then as a drag queen."

What about the idea, widely held by straight people, that all gay males cross-dress or want to cross-dress? "Most gay men don't like drag. It irritates them. Drag queens irritate them."

Then Gavin says with great dignity, "I am a stereotypical faggot"—words most gays find offensive and demeaning. But he uses them to make a point. "I resent the gay movement's turning away from us, finding drag queens humiliating, an embarrassment." There's sadness in his voice when he says, "We've been shoved aside."

DON Meet Don. He's divorced, has three grown children, and is definitely straight. He also cross-dresses. Not that you'd ever guess it if you were a student in one of his classes. Don is a sociology professor at a well-known college. Don is ruggedly masculine looking and he wears strictly male clothes when he's in the classroom.

Over a cup of coffee in his book-lined study Don explains, "I was always fascinated by gender and gender role playing. Curiosity, playing the role of a girl in a skit, losing a bet or taking a dare, even dressing as a girl on Halloween can get you thinking about cross-dressing. And it's an old theatrical tradition. I used to read about vaudeville when I was a kid. Women came out on stage in tuxedos and sang. There were men who performed on stage dressed as women. Audiences loved it. They still do. Stand-up comics and comedians cross-dress. Actors cross-dress in movies. Look at Dustin Hoffman in *Tootsie*. Of course, I'm not an actor. I'm a TV [transvestite]."

Don took us back to the beginning, telling us how he was fascinated by cross-dressing as a child and began putting on women's clothes secretly in his bedroom when he was a teenager. "I didn't understand it then. I don't understand it now. The urge to cross-dress feels like a force. Because I couldn't stop cross-dressing, by seventeen I was convinced I must really be gay even though I never had sexual fantasies about boys. I only thought about girls. Back then there was a theory that some people were latent homosexuals. It's a theory that hardly anybody takes seriously anymore. Latent homosexuals were supposed to be men who seemed straight and believed themselves to be straight—but delve deeply enough into their psyche and you'd discover potential homosexuality, secretly affecting them even though they were attracted to women. Of course, this theory makes no sense. Accept it and you could say anybody was a latent homosexual. It's unprovable. I wasn't a latent anything. I was and am strongly, powerfully heterosexual. I love women."

Does his heterosexuality make Don a rarity in the world of cross-dressers? "No way. The vast majority of men who cross-dress, maybe as many as ninety percent, are straight.''

Now that's a startling revelation! Most people think gays and gays only dress up in women's clothes. "Then most people are wrong. Cross-dressing is falsely associated with homosexuality because homosexuality and the desire for female identity are linked in the public's mind. But they're separate phenomena. Cross-dressing is a lot more complicated and a lot more widespread than the public realizes.''

And Don told us a story. "Let's start with a boy— we'll call him John. He's eleven, twelve, maybe thirteen years old. He finds girls very attractive. He likes the soft, silky feel of their clothes, especially stockings and underwear. He discovers that he gets an erection from putting on girls' clothes." (Girls, happily free to wear jeans, sneakers, and floppy sport sox, will find this passion for itchy nylon puzzling.) "He enjoys masturbating in front of a mirror while wearing girls' clothes. John is a typical straight young transvestite. Gays who cross-dress don't find cross-dressing sexually exciting, which is why they don't like to be called transvestites.''

We remembered the way Gavin described himself. A female impersonator, a drag queen. He gets no sexual thrills out of dressing as Glenda. She's a role he plays, a character he's created.

Don went on with his story. "Years pass. John is all grown up. Sometimes he finds dressing in women's clothes sexually exciting, sometimes he doesn't. But he continues to cross-dress anyway.''

Why? "For some men it's a gesture of defiance, a form of rebellion. For others it's a dangerous game, filled with secrecy and risk. Still others see it as a way of bringing color and flamboyance into their lives. John finds it soothing and comforting."

At this point Don launched into an elaborate lecture filled with words like "fetishism" and "exhibitionism" until we shouted, "Hey, we're not writing a textbook on psychology!"

"Sorry, I am a professor."

The lecture ended and Don answered the rest of our questions. For one thing, we learned there is no one pattern for TVs. Being human, each is a unique individual. Transvestites run the gamut from men who cross-dress once a month or so, wearing only one or two pieces of women's clothing, to men who cross-dress every day or every chance they get. Some cross-dress only in total privacy. Others share their cross-dressing with one or two other people. Some go in for full female regalia including a handbag, a wig, and makeup. Some meet in groups and go to restaurants or shopping malls, or take vacations together. Some wear women's underwear beneath their business suits, uniforms, or greasy overalls, depending on their line of work. Some form clubs and support groups. So do their wives and girlfriends.

What are they like, these straight men dressed as women who most people automatically assume are gay when they spot them in public? Are they gentle? Are they "sissies"? No. Usually they're very tough, very macho men. Many are happily married and have kids. And perhaps because they're aggressive and competitive many also succeed at their work. There are top lawyers, doctors, business executives, judges, military personnel, and police officers who are transvestites.

Don claims, "I know of a senator and a former presidential candidate who cross-dress. People would be amazed to know how common transvestism is. Some macho-type men cross-dress because it's their way of allowing themselves to be soft and vulnerable. All day while they're at work they have to be tough and strong. In their families they're the responsible one others lean on. I have a powerful friend who becomes the stereotype of the docile person when he cross-dresses. Cross-dressing transforms TVs. It's an escape from a cold, cruel, ruthless world. Dressed as a woman they can cry. Dressed in men's clothing they have to be the most masculine of men. They have to be Superman."

And women? Do women cross-dress? "At one time some did. Nowadays women can wear just about anything men wear and nobody considers it cross-dressing. Fashions change. Take earrings. When I was a teenager earrings were for women only. If a man wore them he was cross-dressing. It was an outrageous thing to do. Not now. Earrings are an accepted style of male dress these days. Maybe someday high heels and evening gowns will be socially acceptable clothing for men. A crazy idea? You never can tell."

The coffee pot's empty. Don has one last thing to say. "Look, cross-dressing isn't violent or sadistic and it doesn't hurt others. Ask people to remember that."

ANGELA Meet Angela. Angela doesn't wear glamorous clothes very often. Like most women, she dresses simply and casually most of the time. But there was a time when she had to practice how to look feminine in women's clothes. Angela is a TS (transsexual). Or, to put it more accurately, a post-operative male-to-female transsexual. Okay, we can hear you saying, "This has got to be a gay man who had a sex-change operation because he wanted to be a woman and get straight men."

Angela's response to this? "Before the change I was married to a woman I loved deeply for ten years. I wasn't at all attracted to men. I never had sex with a man. I still feel the same. I am attracted only to women. Sexual preference had nothing to do with my decision to have surgery."

Before we go any farther we should tell you that not only is Angela an intelligent, compassionate person who spends a lot of her free time trying to help other transsexuals, she's also highly responsible. She'd be the first to tell you that the hormonal treatments and the surgery needed to alter someone's genitals and secondary sexual characteristics (facial hair, breasts, etc.) are potentially very dangerous. The procedure's also painful and controversial. It does not transform a person's genetic structure or reproductive system and for this reason some doctors consider it merely an elaborate form of plastic surgery. The psychological adjustments that have to be made are huge. So not surprisingly, very few people even contemplate undergoing the surgery, and even fewer go through with it. On the whole the surgery seems to be more successful for female-to-male transsexuals than for male-to-female ones.

"But for me it was the right thing to do," says Angela. "All my life I was convinced my body was the wrong body for the self inside. I felt like my body was a birth defect. Every morning I'd get out of bed, look at myself in the mirror, and say, 'I wish I'd been born a woman.' My being a man was a biological goof-up. Something went wrong somewhere. Nature made a mistake. Before the change I was desperately unhappy. Now, even though life still has plenty of problems, at least I have a life. My body and mind are in sync. We're one. I'm complete.''

Are transsexuals ever taken for drag queens when they cross-dress? "During the period we call cross-living, before surgery, yes. Long before surgery transsexuals have to learn to look like and act like they belong in their chosen gender. Male-to-female transvestites have to learn to walk, stand, and sit like a woman, to speak like a woman, to get their hair styled in a feminine way. The one group they're advised to stay away from is teenagers. Teenagers are so sensitive to gender differences they can spot transsexuals better than anyone else. Teens always read them as gays.''

And what happens when they do? "Usually nothing. Sometimes name-calling, 'queer' and 'faggot.' But sometimes it's worse. Running into a crowd of hostile gay bashers is one of the hazards of cross-dressing.'' Angela shakes her head. "Why are people so cruel?''

So that's Glenda/Gavin, Don, and Angela. We hope they've cleared up some misconceptions: that most gays cross-dress or want to cross-dress; that straight men never cross-dress except as a joke; that gays wish they could change their gender; that nobody straight would ever dream of a gender change; that common stereotypes reflect reality and help us see people clearly.

6 The Sin of Sodom

"You're not allowed to admit you could be—
not even the possibility—not even spoken
about."   —ADRIENNE E., AGE 17

When Beth was preparing for her bas
mitzvah, the ceremony that marks a Jewish girl's
passage into young womanhood, she confided to her
rabbi the belief that she might be a lesbian.

The rabbi, an old family friend, seemed sympathetic and concerned. He told Beth it was just a
phase that she was going through, and that she
would soon get over it. Beth does not recall the
rabbi ever mentioning the subject again. In fact, she
thinks he sort of avoided her after that. For Beth,
now twenty-two and a lesbian activist, it was not a
passing phase.

Kenny says with a smile that he was attending
Methodist youth group meetings from the time he
was born. His family was very involved in the Methodist church of their small midwestern town. Kenny
was one of his church's most active youth leaders.
He remembers, with warmth and affection, long bus

trips to conferences and regional meetings, with lots of singing and good fellowship.

When he was sixteen Kenny confided to his minister, a man he knew well and trusted, the fear that he might be gay. As with Beth's rabbi, the minister seemed sympathetic and concerned. He told Kenny not to worry, it was a passing phase and he would soon get over it. The subject never came up again.

Kenny is now twenty. Upon his graduation from high school he left his hometown and is now living in Chicago with his male lover. It wasn't a passing phase for him either.

Both Beth and Kenny insist that they are still "religious," though neither has attended any formal religious services since they left their parents' homes. Both feel that they were let down or abandoned by the religions that were supposed to nurture and help them. There had been no hostility, merely embarrassment and the feeling that neither the rabbi nor the minister knew what to do or say. Beth and Kenny don't feel that there is any place for them in the formal religious structure that they grew up with.

Beth's and Kenny's experiences are comparatively happy ones. Mark just laughs out loud when asked if he had ever talked to his pastor about his homosexuality. Mark's family were evangelicals, and the church was central to their lives.

"If I told my pastor I was gay he'd have thrown me out of his study, and then denounced me in front of the whole congregation. To him being a homosexual was the worst sin in the world. Worse than murder, I swear.

"Look at Jim Bakker of the PTL. [In 1987 Jim Bakker, an extremely popular TV evangelist, was involved in a highly publicized scandal in which both sex and money played a role.] When he was accused of seducing a teenaged church secretary—a girl— people were willing to forgive him. When it turned out he was misappropriating millions of dollars that had been collected for missionary work, people were willing to forgive him. But when it was rumored that he was also a homosexual, that was it. That was the unforgiveable sin. There was no way I could talk to my pastor. When I was old enough to get out of the church, I got out. And I stayed out."

Karen went to a Catholic school. She knew she was gay, or at least "different," from about the time she was twelve. She remembers that the kids at her school were always telling "fag jokes." In class one of the students said, "All the fags should be put on an iceberg, or shot into outer space." Everyone, including the teacher, laughed. Karen does not remember a single incident when a member of the faculty, lay or religious, said anything about the jokes or the other cruel and cutting remarks. Students and faculty alike seemed to share the same viciously anti-homosexual attitudes. There was no one in her school she felt she could talk to.

Karen was sixteen when she first went to a gay bar. Much to her surprise, she saw two of the female teachers from her school there. Instead of greeting her they tried to avoid her. The teachers knew that all Karen had to do was hint that they were lesbians, and they would be out of their jobs.

"I was raised to be a good Catholic girl," Karen

says. "I haven't been to church in years. You know, I miss it sometimes. I really do. But I look around and I see members of the Catholic hierarchy leading the fight against gay and lesbian rights. I read the pronouncements from Rome on homosexuality, and I know that the Church doesn't want me as I am. The Church wants me to be something else, something I'm not, something I can't be."

Karen has been attending meetings of Dignity, an organization of lesbian and gay Catholics that has been challenging official Church positions on homosexuality. Karen still considers herself a Catholic and hopes the Church will change. But she does not expect change to come soon.

Jack had the greatest difficulties of all, for Jack is a devout Mormon and a homosexual. The attitude of the Mormon church toward homosexuality is as severe as that of any religious group in the country. To the Mormon church, homosexuality is a "deep, dark sin." The church not only opposes gay rights in any form, it even regrets that there are places in the United States where sexually active homosexuals cannot be arrested. This is viewed as "another evidence of the deterioration of society."

Moreover, the Mormons view homosexuality as an immoral choice, not an inborn orientation. It is also seen as something that is "curable" with aid and sufficient "self will." Writing about curing homosexuality, Spencer W. Kimball, who was until his death leader of the Mormons, used the quote, "The first and greatest victory is to conquer yourself; to be conquered by yourself is of all things most shameful and vile." Ironically, the quote comes from the Greek philosopher Plato, who celebrated homosexual love in his writings.

Jack is an eighth-generation Mormon, and grew up in a small town in Utah "ninety-seven percent Mormon." Church and family provided a warm and supportive atmosphere for him when he was very young.

Yet Jack sensed that he was somehow "different" from the time he was in third or fourth grade. In school boys and girls were separated at that age. Homosexuality was a subject that simply was not discussed in Mormon homes or schools. No one said it was wrong, no one said it existed. "Yet from the age of twelve I had engaged in sexual activity with several of the boys in my ward [congregation] and in my neighborhood on many occasions."

When he was seventeen Jack confessed his sexual activities to his bishop and was sent for counseling to a Mormon social service agency. At this point he still believed what he had been told about homosexuality being "learned behavior" that could, with "self will," be "unlearned."

For a little over two years Jack remained celibate, but then the "old feelings" came back, and quickly so did the old sexual activities. Once again he went to his bishop and was told it was just a "phase" he was going through. He was given the "same counsel and advice plus the usual prayer, scripture reading, and fasting." He was also sent to another Mormon social service agency.

He was urged to start dating, and he met a girl and became engaged. But Jack couldn't sustain the relationship. He became uncomfortable, and withdrew. Within a few months he had broken off the engagement.

Jack says that he is "awestruck" at the number of gay Mormons. There are half a dozen gay bars in Salt Lake City alone, frequented primarily by Mormon men who are married, have children, and teach Sunday school. "I hated to see the hypocrisy," he says. It was a style of life that Jack would not, or could not, lead.

Finally, after a long struggle, Jack asked to be excommunicated from the Mormon church.

He says that the most traumatic time of his life came in April 1987. "I met an individual who had faithfully served the Lord and kept all the commandments for nearly a decade, and he was still a homosexual. I began to understand for myself that 'homosexuality' was a great deal more than sexual activity. I admitted to myself that I am a child of God and I am a homosexual. It was a rude awakening when I discovered that I did not choose to be a homosexual . . . I felt deceived and betrayed."

Yet Jack still considers himself a Mormon. His two older brothers, both straight, have long since left the church. Jack, though excommunicated, still attends a Mormon church in California. He can't participate in the service because he has been excommunicated, and he has not been made to feel terribly welcome. But he goes anyway.

He tried to attend meetings of Affirmation, an unofficial group for gay Mormons, but he didn't like it and regards it as an "apostate church." At one meeting he was very distressed at what he took to be anger toward the church and President Kimball. Jack still thinks of a brief meeting with President

Kimball as the "high point of my life." He recalls, "As he entered the room and I rose to my feet without thought, I sensed his tenderness and love and knew in my heart he was a Prophet of God." This is the same President Kimball, Jack knows, who wrote of homosexuality as a "deep dark sin" and a "curable" illness.

Jack has even considered becoming celibate if the Mormons would respect him as a person, but he feels it doesn't work that way. The church is family oriented, and there is no comfortable place for single people, particularly single people who are known to be homosexual (albeit celibate ones). Jack is lonely. He misses the family he can't have and the church that has no place for him. He has thrown himself into family genealogy, a particular Mormon passion. In his researches Jack has found one unmarried uncle in his family, who was placed in a mental institution. "Was he gay?" Jack wonders. "Did the tension between being gay and being a Mormon cause a breakdown? . . . I am struggling through the process of being gay and being Mormon."

"Judge not that ye be not judged," Jack says.

Religion is very important in the lives of many lesbians and gay men for a variety of reasons. First, homosexuals are born into the same sort of religious or nonreligious backgrounds as everybody else. There is absolutely no reason to believe that more lesbians and gays are born into families of nonbelievers or nominal believers than into families that are deeply religious. They grow up with the same religious beliefs, the same religious needs, as the rest of us. Indeed, for some young homosexuals the religious needs can be unusually strong. In addition to facing all the normal traumas of adolescence, they face the extra trauma of being "different." For many teens a church or synagogue can be a source of comfort, inspiration, guidance, even a good place to meet other teens. Most homosexual teenagers feel cut off from these benefits. All too often they feel they have been met with embarrassed silence, lack of understanding, or outright hostility. They are left out, pushed out, and deeply hurt.

Even if you aren't particularly religious, or religious at all, your attitude—everybody's attitude—toward homosexuality has been shaped by the Judeo-Christian religious tradition. Organized religious groups are often very active in public matters affecting homosexuals. Most of this activity would have to be considered hostile. For example, the Roman Catholic church has been one of the strongest and most effective opponents of laws that extend civil-rights protections to homosexuals. Fundamentalist Christian churches often campaign very successfully to have books sympathetic to homosexuals, like this one, banned from school and public libraries.

Where does the hostility come from? The Judeo-Christian tradition has been strongly anti-homosexual for thousands of years. It begins with the Old Testament and the famous story of God's destruction of the city of Sodom. The story is told in Genesis. God has heard of the sinfulness of the city of Sodom and the city of Gomorrah. He sends two angels to Sodom to see if they can find ten good men from among the city's residents. If only that small number can be found, God declares, the cities will be saved. Otherwise they will be destroyed.

The two angels appear as men, enter Sodom, and are taken as guests into the house of one good man, Lot. But the entire male population of the city then surrounds Lot's house, demanding: "Bring them out to us, that we may know them."

In Hebrew, the language of the Old Testament, the verb "to know" was often used in the sense of "to have intercourse with." The next morning, at the urging of the angels, Lot and his family flee the city, and God rains down fire and brimstone on Sodom and Gomorrah.

Recently a few biblical scholars have questioned whether the verb "to know" actually had a sexual meaning in the story of Sodom. That, however, is very much a minority view. Reading the story over, we found it impossible to deny the traditional interpretation, that sex is just exactly what the men of Sodom had in mind. Over the centuries "Sodomite" has become a virtual synonym for male homosexual.

The second major Old Testament reference to homosexuality comes in Leviticus. This book contains a long list of "thou shalt nots" and the penalties, usually severe, to be imposed on those who disobey. Male homosexuality is clearly condemned as a sin, and a serious one, for the prescribed penalty is death.

So the Jews of biblical times were sternly opposed to male homosexuality, and if you are given a sentence here and a phrase there from the Bible it can be made to sound like the most heinous of sins. But when we look at the entire Old Testament and the other ancient Jewish traditions, it becomes obvious that male homosexuality was just one of many, many practices that were severely condemned. It wasn't one that the Jews themselves were particularly concerned about, regarding it primarily as a vice of non-Jews, or as part of the practice of an idolatrous religion. The practice of some Middle Eastern religions in biblical times may have involved male and female prostitution.

Let's go back to the story of Sodom. What is being specifically condemned here is not the kind of homosexual act that takes place between two consenting individuals. What is being condemned here is homosexual *rape*. The mob is threatening to gang rape a couple of strangers. Everyone, gay and straight alike, would agree that's a sin and a crime.

There are a couple of other references to the story of Sodom and Gomorrah in the Old Testament. Sins such as oppression of the poor, pride, gluttony, laziness, and idolatry are listed as reasons for the destruction of the cities—but homosexuality isn't.

In the New Testament there are two references to the story of Sodom and Gomorrah. Here, the chief sin of these notorious towns appears to be inhospitality. Once again, homosexuality isn't even mentioned.

Leviticus, as we said, has a long list of laws—on what to eat, how to reap a field, how to treat illness, and when and with whom to have sexual intercourse. Male homosexuality is punishable by death, but so are adultery and fornication. So, by the way, is disobedience to parents. These were all equally grave sins.

Time and new traditions have greatly softened

and changed the stern laws of the ancient Hebrews, but some have softened more than others. If one of your male teachers was found to be having an affair with his neighbor's wife, he might have trouble with his own family—but would he be driven out of his job and be shunned by people who he had once regarded as friends? We seriously doubt it. But that's exactly what might happen if he was discovered to be a homosexual.

If a boy and girl in your class are sleeping together—that's fornication—do other members of the class call them names in the hall, or scrawl insults on their lockers? Once again, we doubt it. But that's what would happen if the couple happened to be homosexual and everybody else knew it. By the way, the Old Testament has nothing to say about female homosexuality. Either the ancient Hebrews didn't know it existed, or they didn't care.

And we leave it to you to decide what your punishment should be for the last time you talked back to your parents.

The New Testament contains three clear references to homosexuality. All are in the letters by or attributed to St. Paul. In Corinthians homosexuality is listed in a catalog of sins that includes such other sins as adultery, greed, and drunkenness.

Some biblical scholars have argued that Paul is not condemning homosexuality in general, but only that form of homosexuality that would have been most familiar to him. Paul lived in a place and time dominated by the culture of the ancient Greeks and Romans. As we will see in Chapter 7, homosexual relations between adult males and boys were not only common, but widely accepted in the Greco-Roman world. This type of homosexuality, which we call pederasty, would undoubtedly have been what Paul had seen most often.

The condemnation of homosexual activity in Timothy may be even more specific. Here homosexuality appears to be linked with kidnapping and the use of young male slaves for sexual purposes.

The most extensive discussion of homosexuality in the Old or New Testament comes in Romans 1:26–27. Since much of modern Christian opposition to homosexuality is based on this passage, we will quote it in full: from the Revised Standard Version.

"Therefore, God gave them up to dishonorable passions. For not only did their females exchange natural intercourse for that which is against nature, but also males, leaving natural intercourse with females, lusting in their desire for one another, males working shame with males and receiving the punishment within themselves which their falsehood necessitated."

A couple of things about these verses strike one immediately. First, they contain what appears to be a *clear* reference to female homosexuality—the only one in the Bible. Even here there has been a dispute. Some scholars have argued that the reference is not to female homosexuality but to certain positions of heterosexual intercourse deemed deviate by pious Jews—"females exchange natural intercourse for that which is against nature."

The second thing that stands out to anyone reading all of Paul's letters is that the passage referring to homosexuality isn't very long, and that homosexuality is merely an example of a much greater problem. Paul speaks of many "crimes." In the very next verse he refers to "whisperers and scandal mongers, hateful to God, insolent, arrogant and boastful . . ." It is impossible to escape the feeling that the "sin" of homosexuality did not loom nearly as large in biblical times as it does today.

Some gay Christians have argued that Paul is not talking about them. The various crimes or sins listed by Paul are the result of denying God. Indeed, it is the denial of God rather than the specific sin of homosexuality, or any other specific sin, that Paul is really talking about in Romans. The gay Christians say that they do not deny God.

Many gay Christians and some biblical scholars insist Paul is preaching against homosexuality that is "against nature"; that is, homosexual acts by individuals who are not by nature homosexual. Examples might be the homosexual prostitute who is not really homosexual but simply does it for the money, or the individual who forces or coerces another into a homosexual act that he does not really want. Paul, they argue, has nothing to say about loving and consensual relationships between two individuals who are by nature homosexual.

Professor Robin Scroggs, of the Union Theological Seminary, addresses the problem from the point of view of a biblical scholar in his book *The New Testament and Homosexuality*. "Despite the general language Paul, with regard to the statement about male homosexuality, must have had, *could only have had*, pederasty in mind. That Paul uses here the argument from nature [that is, homosexuality is against nature] might mean, of course, that he would have made the same judgement about *any* form of homosexuality. No one can legitimately conclude, however, that he would have done so. We just do not know. What he would have said about the contemporary model of adult/adult mutuality in same-sex relationships, we shall also never know. I am not sure it is even useful to speculate."

So there is a genuine controversy over what the Bible has to say about homosexuality. But it would be very wrong of us to leave the impression that most or even many Christian leaders and scholars have much doubt about just what the position of the Bible and the Judeo-Christian tradition is and should be toward any sort of homosexuality: It is a sin.

In 1986 the Vatican issued a long letter on the subject of homosexuality. Many non-Catholic Christians doubtless agreed with the Vatican letter, which is quite clear that homosexual activity is not a morally acceptable option.

There is, said the letter, "a clear consistency within the Scriptures themselves on the moral issue of homosexual behavior. The Church's doctrine regarding this issue is thus based not on isolated phrases for facile theological argument but on the solid foundation of a constant biblical testimony. The community of faith today is unbroken continuity with Jewish and Christian communities within which the ancient Scriptures were written, and continues to be nourished by those same Scriptures and by the spirit of truth whose word they are. It is likewise essential to recognize that the Scriptures are not properly understood when they are interpreted in a way which contradicts the Church's living tradition."

But despite the fact that most modern religious

groups reject them, or at least their life-style, there are still many, many gay religious people. What do they do?

There are gay churches. The largest is the Universal Fellowship of Metropolitan Community Churches. It was begun in Los Angeles in 1968 by the Reverend Troy Perry, who had been thrown out of the fundamentalist church in which he had been pastor for his homosexuality.

Currently the Universal Fellowship has about two hundred churches throughout the world with some thirty thousand members. Though the church is open to all people it is regarded, quite accurately, as primarily a church for lesbians and gay men.

The small Faith Temple describes itself as "a non-denominational, Bible-believing church. We take the New Testament as our rule for faith and order. More specifically, we are Evangelical, Charismatic, and Liberationist."

Faith Temple is made up mainly of black gay men from fundamentalist backgrounds. Temple founder James S. Tinney has written: "What does it mean to be 'saved'? It means to be *delivered* not from homosexuality (you cannot be anything other than what God has made you)—but delivered from guilt, from the penalty and punishment that sinners deserve and from fear and powerlessness."

In a personal testimony on the subject of salvation, published by the Faith Temple, one member writes: "When I instead place Jesus Christ at the center of my existence and allow his love, truth, and goodness to flow through me, I find the power to live and be myself. And it is that permission God gives me to 'be myself'—even as he helps me become a better 'me'—that is one of the great joys of salvation."

Most religious lesbians and gay men do not join gay churches; rather, they attempt to maintain some sort of relationship with the religion into which they were born. For Jews there is the New Jewish Agenda. A brochure from that organization proclaims: "As Jews, we know how important it is to have our differences respected, not to be forced to hide or asked to change. Our understanding of the concerns of lesbians and gay men is rooted both in our sense of justice and in our history. We know what it means to have to conceal important parts of one's identity in order to hold a job, live where one chooses, obtain a travel visa, or simply exist without daily threats of violence."

Dignity, an organization of gay and lesbian Catholics and their supporters that came into being in 1969, has recently been engaged in a difficult and often highly publicized struggle with the Church hierarchy. "Growth has been rapid almost in direct proportion to oppression," says a Dignity letter. The letter reflects that the organization's attempt to open the church to lesbian and gay Catholics "has not been smooth or comfortable, but then no one ever said that being an active Christian would be easy."

Dignity's statement of position says: "We believe that gay men and lesbian women can express their sexuality in a manner that is consonant with Christ's teaching. We believe that all sexuality should be exercised in an ethically responsible and unselfish way."

Kinship is a small but very active and lively group

of gay men and lesbians who were or are Seventh
Day Adventists. The Adventists are among the most
conservative religious groups in the country and immediately kick out any active and open homosexuals. Some members of Kinship still regard themselves as Adventists, while others come from
Adventist backgrounds and look upon Kinship as
more of a support group for former Adventists who
happen to be homosexuals. Kinship also attracts
gays and lesbians from other conservative religious
groups, who share similar backgrounds and experiences.

And there is, of course, Affirmation, the group for
gay and lesbian Mormons that we already mentioned.

These are just some of the organizations that attempt to help gay men and lesbian women deal with
their religious needs, in the face of general hostility
or indifference from organized religion.

While hostility would fairly describe the attitude
of most religions toward the actively homosexual individual, particularly if that individual openly proclaims that he or she is both gay and proud, at least
the subject is now open for discussion. Ten or
twenty years ago that would have been simply unthinkable.

Among Jews the Orthodox remain firmly opposed
to any accommodation to homosexual behavior. In
New York City, for example, Orthodox Jews have
often joined with conservative Christians to try and
block gay rights legislation. But openly homosexual
Jews have been accepted in some Reform, Recon-
structionist, and even Conservative congregations.

The very liberal Unitarian Universalist church is

completely open to homosexuals. A gay Unitarian Universalist wrote, "We have no dogma, believe in neither sin nor hell, marry same-sex partners, and ordain both women and homosexuals into our ministry."

The Quakers, another religious group that traditionally has favored personal liberty over any form of authority or dogma, has also been very open to homosexuals.

In the larger, more mainstream Protestant churches, the place of the homosexual in the church is likely to be the subject of intense and emotional controversy at major church assemblies and meetings. It's a subject that comes up in a variety of ways, is studied, reported on, restudied, and rereported on without any firm or generally accepted conclusions.

The Episcopal church is probably the most liberal of the mainstream American churches regarding homosexuals. A number of leading churchmen have stated that a loving relationship between two adults of the same sex is "natural" and not contrary to God's will. Not all Episcopalians agree by any means, but sentiment for gays and lesbians in the church runs strong.

The Methodists, the Presbyterians, and the United Church of Christ have all had reports and discussions on the issue, with meetings and conferences usually sharply split between liberals and conservatives.

Officially the Roman Catholic church still regards homosexuality as a "moral disorder." Homosexual Catholics are often urged to try and correct this "disorder" through counseling and prayer. But there is also a recognition on the part of many in the church that there is such a thing as an inborn and "incurable" homosexual orientation. Such Catholics are advised to adopt celibacy. Indeed, there are homosexually oriented but celibate priests, nuns, and brothers.

An often stated Catholic position is "God loves the sinner, but not the sin." It is possible for a homosexual Catholic, even an active one, to remain within the church, just as it is possible for those who commit adultery to remain. Even the very severe Vatican letter on homosexuality acknowledges that homosexual persons are "often generous and giving of themselves." The focus of controversy today is those homosexual Catholics and their supporters, like the members of Dignity, who openly campaign to make same-sex relationships an acceptable life-style in and out of the church.

The more conservative Christian churches regard any form of homosexual activity and orientation not only as sinful, but as a correctable or "curable" disorder. They support special ministries or other groups that promise to change homosexuals to heterosexuals. These groups are often run by individuals who label themselves "ex-gay"—that is, reformed or "cured" homosexuals. Much success has been claimed by such groups. But is this success real or illusory?

We have already looked at the case of Jack, the devout Mormon who was unable to change his homosexuality despite extensive counseling from Mormon social service agencies.

When writing about homosexuality, Spencer Kimball claimed great success for the Mormon programs, but the two "testimonial" letters of gratitude he cites are strange.

The first came from a young man who had engaged in a homosexual act out of "curiosity" when he was only ten years old. But the memory of it very much bothered him. When he finally confessed, "My kindly bishop cleared the slate," and he felt "well and clean."

The second came from a young man who was described only as having "waded in deep waters." He said that with the help of the church he had adjusted "during the past year," although there "are still struggles."

Neither of these testimonials represents evidence of a great "cure" or "change." In the first, a young man was made to feel forgiven for a brief and probably meaningless encounter while still a child. In the second, we are given no indication of how strong the young man's homosexual drive was, and in any case, only a year—and a troubled one at that —had gone by since his "change."

A major scandal was uncovered in a program, backed by the Seventh Day Adventists, that promised to change homosexuals to heterosexuals. The director of the program, who called himself an "ex-gay," was found to be sexually exploiting some of those who came to him for help.

One young man who had entered the program hoping to be cured later reported: "I saw many good people on an earnest search being hurt by irresponsible psychology, not to mention widespread sexual exploitation. One by one we observed that it was not possible to change our orientation . . .

"I had gone to my church for the help I needed.

What I had received was abuse, unproven psychology, and a counselor who needed more help than I did."

A dropout from one of the other religiously backed "ex-gay" programs states: "We prayed and pleaded with God for deliverance from our homosexual nature. . . . Although I was completely open and honest before God, my homosexual feelings remained. . . . There are some gay Christians still claiming to be 'ex-gay' but these statements are being made by faith as they continue to suppress their homosexual feelings. . . ."

Many claims of "cures" or "changes" are still made by religiously backed treatment and counseling programs. However, as with faith healing, the evidence of success is not statistics and carefully controlled studies but unsupported testimonials and a couple of scientifically worthless reports. There are few, if any, follow-ups on individual cases to find out how long the "cure" lasts.

There isn't even a clear idea of what a successful "change" is supposed to be. Is a person driven by guilt and fear into celibacy and loneliness changed for the better? Is the person trapped in a loveless and unsatisfactory marriage somehow fulfilling God's plan? Is the spouse in such a marriage, who is equally trapped, also part of this plan? Somehow we doubt it.

There is no evidence to suggest that the religiously based attempts to change deep-seated homosexual orientation have been any more successful than those of psychologists and psychiatrists. That is to say, they have not been very successful at all.

There are no easy solutions to the dilemma that homosexuality presents to religious groups today. At one time the homosexual in America was so tightly closeted that he or she was not a problem that had to be dealt with very often. That is no longer the case today. Homosexuality is a major issue, in some cases *the* major issue, facing religious groups in America today. And it is likely to remain so for many years to come.

7
From Plato to Stonewall

> "I am Hispanic and Hispanics admire macho behavior. Being gay is considered sissy stuff. When I said in history class I was gay two girls fainted. But some people respected me for having the courage to come out so publicly."
> —CARLOS S., AGE 18

As far as anyone can tell, homosexuals have always been a part of human society. Attitudes toward them have varied a great deal throughout history. Sometimes homosexuality has been regarded as a perfectly natural, acceptable, even desirable human activity. Other times it has been denounced as a vile sin and dangerous perversion. But no matter the attitude of the majority, homosexuals have always been here.

Homosexuality has existed in practically every society that we know of, from the Polynesian to the Eskimo. It is far, far too vast a subject to be covered in a brief chapter. We are going to concentrate on homosexuality in Western history, and mostly in recent Western history, to look at the ideas and events that have most strongly shaped our attitudes and actions today. But in order to understand our attitudes today we have to first go back several thousand years.

As we have seen, the Jews of biblical times disapproved strongly of homosexuality, in part at least because it was common among their "idolatrous" neighbors and enemies. The early Christians adopted the same view and also disapproved strongly of homosexuality. But the subject does not appear to have been an overriding concern to either Jews or Christians of biblical times.

For the ancient Greeks, however, homosexuality was a way of life. The most common form of homosexuality among the Greeks, or at least the one that they wrote about most frequently, was the relationship between an adult male and a young man or boy. Today we would call the practice *pederasty* (pederast means, literally, lover of boys), and it is frowned upon even in the gay community, in the same way that a relationship between an adult male and a very young girl is frowned upon among heterosexuals. While homosexual acts between consenting adults are not illegal in over half of the states in the United States, and laws against such acts are rarely enforced in most other states, pederasty is considered child molesting, and it's illegal everywhere.

But for many Greeks it was a natural and expected part of growing up. Among the warlike Spartans it was part of military training. The ideal was for every young man to have an adult lover who would train him in the arts of war. In battle they fought side by side. The boy was the "beloved," the older man the "lover." The presence of the boy was supposed to be a spur to the valiant action of the adult, who would not want to be shamed in his beloved's eyes.

In Athens, where philosophy, poetry, and art flourished, the older man was supposed to be a teacher and role model for the boy, as well as a lover. Greek art and poetry celebrate male beauty. The Greek Olympics were as much a male beauty contest as an athletic contest. All athletes competed in the nude, and no women spectators were allowed at the games.

There were lots of male prostitutes, and handsome slave boys were often used for sexual purposes.

Still, it's not quite accurate to call the Greeks homosexual in the way we generally use the term today. An aristocratic Greek man might be the "beloved" of an older man when he was a boy. When he matured he might become the "lover" of a boy, or of a series of them. Yet typically he would also marry and have a family. So in a sense Greek men were more bisexual than strictly homosexual. Not everyone in Greece approved of this way of life, but at worst it was regarded as a minor vice.

All of this proved to be a great embarrassment to later ages. People in the eighteenth and nineteenth centuries greatly admired the Greeks in many ways, but their sexual practices couldn't even be discussed. Poems and other Greek writings that celebrated homosexual love (and there were plenty of these) were given misleading translations, or if that was impossible simply suppressed. Fig leaves were added to copies of Greek statues. There was talk of "platonic love." The word comes from the Greek philosopher Plato. It was supposed to be a noble, almost spiritual and certainly non-sexual love between two people. Every attempt was made to pretend the Greeks "didn't do it." But the poems, the plays, and hundreds of painted vases show in the most explicit possible way that the Greeks did indeed "do it," and didn't feel one bit guilty about it. And it didn't stop them from creating the most remarkable and productive civilization of the ancient world.

Much less is known about female homosexuality, not only among the Greeks but in all the ancient world—indeed, in all history—until fairly modern times. Among the ancient Greeks the status of women was very low. Women were supposed to stay home, have babies, and shut up. One of the reasons often advanced by the Greeks for taking boys as lovers was that they had better minds than women did.

Not all Greek women stayed home quietly. The term *lesbian* comes from the Greek poetess Sappho who lived on the island of Lesbos. She wrote exotically sensuous poems to women and seems to have been both leader and teacher to a small group of unmarried women, possibly some sort of religious group. Sappho herself was married and had a daughter, but her sexual attraction for other women is undeniable, though in modern times there have been some attempts to deny it.

There were also religious rites connected with the worship of the god Dionysus that were open only to women and almost certainly involved homosexual activity.

While the Romans do not appear to have been as enthusiastic about homosexuality as the Greeks, it was certainly common enough in the Roman world. When young, Julius Caesar is widely believed to have been the "beloved" of King Nicomedes of Bithynia. There was a conservative undercurrent of disapproval of homosexuality in Rome, as there was in Greece. Throughout Caesar's career his relationship with the king of Bithynia was one of the many charges brought against him by his opponents. He was derided as "the queen's rival." But the charge didn't prevent Caesar from becoming the most powerful man in the Roman world. Caesar's soldiers actually admired his sexuality, praising him, perhaps ironically, as "the husband of every woman, the wife of every man." Some of the great warriors of history and legend, such as Achilles and Alexander the Great, had male lovers. Homosexuality did not prevent them from having "manly" warrior virtues.

Caesar's friend Mark Anthony was a great general, but is known today mainly for his long and passionate love affair with Queen Cleopatra of Egypt. Anthony and Cleopatra are supposed to have been one of the great couples of history. Yet when he was young Anthony had picked up the reputation of being little better than a homosexual prostitute for a number of powerful older men. As with Caesar, Anthony's numerous enemies brought the charge against him repeatedly, but it was his relationship with the Egyptian queen that really got him into trouble with the Roman public. The Romans hated foreigners more than they hated homosexuals. Anthony was ultimately defeated by the forces of Octavian, soon to become Augustus Caesar, Rome's first emperor. The emperor was also rumored to have had a homosexual youth.

The careers of the more depraved Roman emperors are often held up as horrible examples of the moral decay that takes hold when homosexuals gain power. The emperor most frequently cited is Caligula, who was murderously insane, disastrously incompetent, and a homosexual. Caligula certainly was all of that, and more, though he was, ironically, assassinated by a man he had publicly ridiculed for being effeminate.

On the other hand, Hadrian was one of the best emperors Rome ever had. He was a competent, energetic administrator, a fine soldier, a humane man (for a Roman emperor), and a homosexual. When Antinous, the emperor's young favorite, drowned in the Nile, not only the emperor but the whole Roman empire went into mourning. The boy was declared to be a god, a city named after him was founded in Egypt, and his birthplace was renamed to honor him. Coins were struck with the boy's likeness on them, and statues of him appeared all over the Roman world.

So prevalent was homosexuality in Roman times that the writer Plutarch felt it necessary to prepare a defense of heterosexuality.

While some, like Julius Caesar, were ridiculed for homosexual behavior, it wasn't a crime, and seemed no more a sin than, say, gluttony. Conservative Romans also connected homosexuality with "foreign," particularly Greek, influence, which they thought weakened the old Roman virtues.

With the triumph of Christianity in the Roman empire it would seem likely that the official attitude toward homosexuality would have become much less tolerant, given the Christians' traditional hostility to the practice. But records from the period are scanty, and we don't really know a lot about how people felt and acted. At least one scholar, John Boswell, has claimed that until about 1150 there was a thriving gay culture in Europe that was at least tolerated by the church. "The early Middle Ages, with few exceptions, had accommodated a great many beliefs and lifestyles with relative ease," he has written.

Then, says Boswell, the attitudes toward homosexuality underwent dramatic changes from "the personal preference of a prosperous minority, satirized and celebrated in popular verse, to a dangerous, antisocial and severely sinful aberration." What had been acceptable in 1100 was by 1300 an activity that could lead to death by burning. Boswell candidly admits that he has no idea what caused this dramatic change. Not all scholars would agree about the early medieval toleration of homosexuality. But of the later persecution there can be no doubt.

In 1307 members of the Knights Templar, an order of military monks that had begun during the Crusades, were suddenly arrested by agents of the powerful king of France, Philip the Fair. The king's real aim was to seize the vast wealth the Templars had collected, for Philip was always in need of money. Among the charges brought against the Templars were sorcery and homosexuality. There may have been some truth to the homosexuality charge. The Templars were knights sworn to celibacy. Though they avoided the company of women, it's not unreasonable to believe that there was some homosexual activity in the group, perhaps a lot of it. The order had also once been centered in the Middle East, where there was a more relaxed attitude toward homosexuality. The Templars had been around since 1128. No one complained about their homosexuality for nearly two hundred years. But by 1307, it had become a serious charge. Templar leaders were tortured to confess, then burned at the stake. The order was broken up and the king of France got the treasure he desired.

Homosexual and bisexual orgies became part of the standard charges leveled against accused heretics and witches throughout the Middle Ages. The charges were certainly exaggerated, if not entirely fabricated. There undoubtedly were homosexuals in Europe during the Middle Ages, but we know of their existence only through the records left by their tormentors.

By the 1700s police reports from a number of European cities indicated the existence of informal networks of gay gathering places. Sometimes the police were met with resistance and defiance. One William Brown, arrested in England in 1726, stated, "There is no crime in making what use I please of my own body."

As in ancient times, much less is known of female homosexuality. In fact, some scholars suggested that female homosexuality wasn't even possible! Women had little freedom to move around and meet on their own. Yet there were also accounts of women who had dressed in men's clothes and actually passed as men for many years.

There is plenty of historical gossip as to who was

and who may have been homosexual. Louis XIII of France probably was gay. He did manage to produce two sons, the famous Louis XIV, who was not gay, and his brother Phillipe Duc d'Orleans, who undoubtedly was, and flamboyantly so, though he did marry and have a large family. The great universal genius Leonardo da Vinci was accused of homosexuality during his lifetime, probably correctly. Though it has been vehemently denied, Michelangelo, who designed St. Peter's in Rome and painted the ceiling of the Sistine Chapel, was also probably gay. The great artist's work celebrates the male body. And he wrote love sonnets to a young man.

Of those homosexuals who were neither aristocratic, rich, or otherwise famous, we know almost nothing.

The French Revolution swept away many old ideas along with the monarchy. The old laws against sodomy were dropped from the Napoleonic Code. Ideally sexuality was to be recognized as an entirely private matter. It didn't always work that way, but for several hundred years France has generally had a more relaxed attitude toward homosexuals than has the English-speaking world, and was often a haven for homosexual exiles from other countries.

Information about homosexuality in early U.S. history is scanty. Since the practice was both illegal and socially disapproved of, most homosexuals remained secretive. When an individual died, families usually burned or otherwise suppressed any letters or other information about homosexuality. Historian Martin B. Duberman almost accidentally ran across a couple of 1826 letters from two antebellum young Southern gentlemen detailing their high-spirited homosexual encounter, for which they felt not the slightest guilt. "Until they [the letters] turned up, few if any scholars (myself included) would have credited the notion that 'carefree' male-male sex ever took place in this country (let alone in the 1820s)—or that off-handed, unemphatic descriptions of it could ever be found," Duberman wrote.

The celebrated nineteenth-century American poet Walt Whitman was gay, though he didn't admit it. When asked directly, he wove fantasies about the illegitimate children he had fathered. For about a century a lot of Whitman scholars denied it, too. They don't anymore. Whitman's contemporary, Herman Melville, certainly had a homosexual predisposition; his writings show that clearly. Whether he was actively homosexual, however, is impossible to know.

By the late nineteenth century there were frequent complaints of "colonies of sexual perverts" in every community of some size in America.

For gays in England the most important and tragic event of the nineteenth century was the trial of Oscar Wilde. Wilde, the author of *The Importance of Being Ernest*, was the wittiest, most flamboyant, and most successful writer of his generation. He was also a homosexual, a fact well known in the artistic and literary circles in which he traveled. His sexual orientation created no real problems for him so long as it remained a relatively private affair.

Wilde, however, had the misfortune to become enamored of an upper-class twerp named Lord Alfred Douglas. This put him in the middle of a fight between Lord Alfred and his eccentric father, the Marquis of Queensberry. Queensberry publicly accused

Wilde of being a "sodomite." Wilde could have, and probably should have, ignored the charge. Instead he sued Queensberry for libel and lost. Wilde was then prosecuted for homosexuality, which was illegal in Victorian England. Once again Wilde could probably have avoided disaster by quietly going into exile in France or Italy, as many others had done before him. But he thought his popularity, wit, and the rightness of his cause made him invulnerable. He had disastrously misjudged the temper of the British public. The first trial ended without a decision. At the second Wilde was convicted and sentenced to two years of hard labor. During the trials Wilde was vilified mercilessly in the press. After the conviction his plays were banned in much of the English-speaking world. The conviction was hailed as a victory for "moral purity" for many years. After his release from prison Wilde, nearly broke but not quite friendless, lived out the last few years of his life in France and Italy. He died in exile in 1900, his life doubtless shortened by the hardships of prison and his fall from public idol to public demon. The savagery that was directed against Wilde, and by implication all gays, sent shock waves through the gay world.

Despite all the persecution, an informal network of bars, clubs, and other meeting places continued to exist in most of the major cities of Europe and America for gay men, and less frequently for lesbians. The network survived periodic police raids, press exposés, and moral crusades.

In 1928 an Englishwoman named Radclyffe Hall published a book called *The Well of Loneliness*, an undisguised lesbian novel. Though the book pleaded

only for "merciful toleration" for the plight of lesbians, which she called "pitiful," it was still met with
howls of moral outrage, particularly in England.
Hall herself was anything but pitiful. Enormously
wealthy, she was able to live life as she pleased.
Still, it took great courage to publish the book at all.
In Britain it was officially labeled as "obscene" because it didn't condemn the lesbian relationship.
But the campaign against the book backfired. It
made *The Well of Loneliness*, which is in fact not a
very good book, famous throughout the world, and
made the subject of lesbianism more public than it
had ever been before. Radclyffe Hall was more for-
tunate than Oscar Wilde.

A far better writer was the American Gertrude
Stein. She wrote about lesbianism honestly, without
any misty metaphors. She also lived openly as a lesbian. But she had to do it in Paris. Such a public life
would have been impossible in America in the early
years of this century. In Paris Stein became the center of a circle of the finest writers and artists of her
generation, among them the Spanish painter Pablo
Picasso and the American writer Ernest Hemingway.

By the early twentieth century homosexuality had
come to be regarded as more of a medical than a
moral problem. In practice, however, it made little
difference whether you were considered a sinner or
a sex pervert. In either case you were regarded as a
danger to society. You were just sent to an institution rather than a prison.

The first moves to have homosexuality recognized
as something other than a sin, serious illness, or
barely tolerated underground activity came in Ger-

many. In 1896 a man by the name of Magnus Hirschfeld wrote that homosexuality was a "deep inner-constituted natural instinct." He rebuked science for its failure to stand for justice and began a campaign to gain full rights for homosexuals. A committee founded by Hirschfeld campaigned to have the laws against homosexuals scrapped, and the campaign gained support from such people as the theologian Martin Buber and the scientist Albert Einstein. In 1919 Hirschfeld founded the Institute for Sex Research, which soon became an internationally respected center for the study of all forms of human sexuality. Berlin in the 1920s was a golden age for gays and lesbians. But that was to end quickly and horribly.

The Nazis, who were rising rapidly to power, had always campaigned on a platform of "moral purity" and denounced homosexuality as a threat to the German nation. Nazi bully boys destroyed the Institute for Sex Research, and leaders in the campaign to reform the laws on homosexuality were thrown into prison. Hirschfeld died in exile. Yet many in the gay community refused to take the Nazi threat seriously. One reason was that Ernst Rohm, head of one of the Nazi militias, was himself a well-known homosexual, and there were many homosexuals in Rohm's private army of goons.

But any illusions about Hitler's intentions toward gays ended on what is called The Night of the Long Knives. On the weekend of June 30 through July 1, 1934, Hitler, Himmler, and Göring had hundreds of their potential rivals within the Nazi movement murdered. The most prominent victim was Ernst Rohm. He was accused of plotting against the regime, and his militia, which was said to be full of "homosexual cliques," was dissolved.

The Nazis pursued a vigorous anti-homosexual campaign. Male homosexuality was a crime in Nazi Germany, and gay men were arrested by the thousands. They were sent to prisons and many ultimately to concentration camps. As the Nazis conquered other European countries, gay men were swept up in their net and sent to the camps.

In the camps prisoners were classified by a set of colored triangles. Jews were made to wear yellow triangles, gypsies brown, etc. Homosexuals were given pink triangles, and along with Jews and gypsies were often singled out for the worst treatment. Some gay groups today have adopted the pink triangle as a symbol of pride.

The number of gays who died in the camps is unknown, for many camp records were destroyed by the Nazis. Estimates range from the tens to the hundreds of thousands. A continuing horror of this horrible era is that the world has failed to recognize that gays were also victims of Nazi persecution. The West German government continued to classify gays as criminals, and thus the few homosexual survivors of the death camps were granted no restitution at all.

Journalism professor Charles-Gene McDaniel described in an article a visit to the notorious Auschwitz death camp in Poland. The guide "slowly recited the list of groups of victims who died awful deaths in that awful place: Jews, Communists, gypsies, scientists and intellectuals, various nationalities and other ethnic groups. But knowingly or unknowingly, this gentle Polish man with the manner of a high-school history teacher ignored, as history has ignored, one major group—homosexuals."

McDaniel then asked if homosexuals were not also prisoners, and the guide admitted that they were. "It was important that others know—and that this well-meaning guide be reminded—that not everyone is willing to ignore the suffering of tens of thousands of the Nazis' victims."

After the Russian revolution, laws against homosexuality in the Soviet Union were dropped. But when Soviet dictator Joseph Stalin consolidated his power, many of the old "morality" laws were reinstated. In 1934 homosexuality once again became a criminal offense in the Soviet Union, and there were mass arrests, mainly of artists, writers, and musicians. Homosexuals were sent to prison or to exile in Siberia. The full story of what happened during the Stalin years is only now beginning to be told. One can expect that the information on the persecution of homosexuals will come out last, for that is always considered a lesser crime.

While life was clearly better for gay men and lesbians in Britain and the United States in the years following World War II, homosexuality was still a crime. Some well-known gays could be more or less open about their sexual preference; the British playwright and actor Noel Coward, for example. Everyone knew Coward was gay, though no one would say so publicly. Coward was not only popular as a writer of sophisticated comedy; his patriotic plays and films made during the war were great morale boosters for the British public.

Yet so long as homosexual behavior remained illegal the laws could be applied capriciously, and sometimes savagely. The British mathematician Alan Turing was one of the real unsung heroes of World War II. He led the successful effort to crack the secrets of the German code machine Enigma. This was one of the greatest espionage coups of the war. Turing was also a brilliant theoretician who laid the groundwork for much modern computer theory. Britain owed a great deal to Alan Turing, but his accomplishments didn't matter at all in the end, for Turing was a homosexual. He was arrested, tried, and convicted and given a choice between going to prison and taking hormone injections that were supposed to "cure" his homosexuality. Turing took the injections, but within a year he committed suicide.

For many gay men and lesbian women in the United States, the war was an eye-opening and liberating experience even though there were strict military regulations against homosexual activity. Gay men were drafted into the army. Lesbians joined the various women's military units. Gay men from small towns suddenly found themselves in the midst of large crowds of men from all over the country, and they discovered that they were not the only ones who were "that way." Rumors of all the lesbians in the women's military were doubtless exaggerated—but not entirely imaginary. A lot of homosexuals who grew up during the war years trace their first sexual experiences back to the time of their military service.

In the years following World War II the United States was in the grip of the Cold War and an anticommunist hysteria that came to be known as McCarthyism—named for Wisconsin Senator Joseph

McCarthy. McCarthy and other like-minded politicians pledged to rid the government, education, the entertainment industry, and all positions of power in America of what they said was a vast communist conspiracy. Homosexuals were somehow supposed to be part of this conspiracy. Even when they were not actually communists homosexuals were denounced as "security risks" because they could be blackmailed or as people who undermined the moral fiber of the nation. Many lost jobs on the mere suspicion of being gay. Many others were driven deeper into a life of deception.

Ironically, McCarthy himself was widely rumored to be a homosexual. The same sort of rumors also swirled around J. Edgar Hoover, head of the FBI and, like McCarthy, a fanatic anticommunist. Rumors about who is, and who might be, are common, and the truth of these rumors is not known. It probably never will be. However, McCarthy's chief assistant, a brilliant and sinister young lawyer named Roy Cohn, definitely was gay. He died of AIDS in 1986. To the end Cohn publicly denied his homosexuality and the nature of the disease that finally killed him. Privately he insisted, and quite possibly believed, that having sex with men did not make him a homosexual!

Still, the first stirrings of what was later to be called "gay liberation" were beginning to be felt. A couple of small and very respectable but openly gay and lesbian organizations were formed. And the underground network of gay bars and clubs continued to expand. Among the small group of writers and artists who were known as "the Beat Generation" there were some who openly celebrated their homosexuality. Allen Ginsberg's long poem "Howl," written in 1955, had quite an impact on college campuses, and there was nothing ambiguous in what the poet had to say about his homosexuality. The publisher of the poem was also prosecuted, unsuccessfully, for obscenity.

The "sexual revolution" of the 1960s ushered in an era of rapid change for gays and lesbians in the United States. Gay life became more and more open and assertive, particularly in places like New York's Greenwich Village and San Francisco's Castro district.

Many lesbians became involved in the growing women's movement and were generally more political than gay men. A charge frequently raised against the women's movement during the 1970s was that all feminists were lesbians. The charge was nonsense, but it could be effective. In 1971 Kate Millett wrote an extremely popular and influential book, *Sexual Politics*. Then she wrote an autobiography in which she revealed that she was bisexual, something her friends already knew. Her honesty cost her any position of leadership within the women's movement.

A watershed moment in what has come to be called the gay liberation movement came on the night of June 27, 1969. The New York police raided a Greenwich Village gay bar called The Stonewall. Bar raids and other forms of harassment were a regular part of police work in New York and other cities. There had been a series of police raids on gay bars in New York over the previous three weeks. But at The Stonewall it was different. Instead of submitting meekly, the patrons and the residents of the heavily gay and lesbian neighborhood fought back. By the end of the weekend The Stonewall had been burned out in the violence, but news of the resistance had swept through the gay community, not only in New York but around the country. The Stonewall riot wasn't the first example of gay resistance to police raids, but it became a symbol. The day is still celebrated as Gay Freedom Day or Gay Pride Day in cities with large gay and lesbian communities.

There were other milestones, some tragic. Harvey Milk, an openly gay businessman, was elected to San Francisco's Board of Supervisors. The charismatic Milk quickly became the most visible and the most effective gay politician in America.

The most outspokenly anti-gay member of the San Francisco Board of Supervisors was an ex-policeman named Dan White. White resigned in 1968, but then changed his mind and asked to be reappointed. Mayor George Moscone refused to do this, and on November 27, 1978, White went to City Hall and shot both Moscone and Milk to death. The first organized reaction of San Franciscans, gay and straight, was a huge candlelight procession to City Hall to honor the slain men, both of whom were extremely popular.

White went on trial for murder. His lawyers put psychiatrists on the stand who testified that the former policeman had suffered from diminished mental capacity because of a "junk food diet." It was called the "Twinkie defense." The real key to the defense, however, was to build sympathy for White by attacking gays. During the jury selection process the defense challenged any potential juror who was homosexual. The strategy worked. The verdict was manslaughter, not murder, and the sentence was seven years and eight months. White actually served just a little over five years for the murder of two of San Francisco's most prominent political figures, though the murder of public officials in California carries a possible death penalty. (In a sense Dan White did suffer the death penalty. Two years after his release from prison he committed suicide. But at the time it looked as if White had gotten away with murder, and that it was "open season" on gays.) When the verdict was announced, thousands of angry marchers descended on City Hall, and there was a riot in which eleven police cars were burned and over a hundred people were sent to the hospital with injuries.

The gay and lesbian community was no longer willing to remain underground and quiet. They wanted—demanded—their rights. Other openly gay and lesbian politicians ran for local office, and some won. A whispering campaign that this or that candidate was homosexual did not immediately doom the candidate to defeat. Many politicians sought the support of the large and increasingly politically active gay community. Gay rights became a respectable political issue in some areas. Twenty or even ten years earlier all of this political activity would have been unthinkable.

Inevitably there was a backlash to this new gay openness, gay pride, and gay political power. At the start of 1977 Dade County—that is, Miami, Florida—passed an ordinance granting full civil rights to gays and lesbians. People could not be discriminated against because of sexual orientation. The ordinance enraged conservative political and religious elements in the state. A campaign to have a referendum to repeal the ordinance was mounted. Its leader was Anita Bryant, a country and western singer and TV spokesperson for Florida orange juice. Backed by conservative religious and political groups, particularly TV evangelists, the Bryant group was able to win a better than 2 to 1 victory, and the law was repealed. Bryant called her group Save the Children, for its basic theme was that gays are child molesters or "recruiters" for homosexuality, and that giving gays equal rights would destroy "family values."

Bryant then moved her campaign to other states and cities that had, or were considering, gay rights legislation. The campaign won victory after victory. In California, State Senator John Briggs sponsored a voter initiative that would expel from the school system all gay men and lesbians, as well as anyone who portrayed homosexuals in a positive light. Once again the cry was "save the children." The Briggs initiative won the support of organizations ranging from the Los Angeles Deputy Sheriffs' Association to the Ku Klux Klan. Early polls indicated that it would win. But this time what had come to be called the Bryant Brigade met organized and effective opposition. Gay spokesmen debated Briggs and exposed the hollowness of his charges of gays as child molesters. The Briggs initiative was defeated by a healthy majority of 58 percent of California voters. At the same time voters in Seattle, Washington, voted overwhelmingly to retain their gay rights law. Anita Bryant, champion of family values, became embroiled in a very public divorce and then went into eclipse. The movement against gay rights, which had, for a time, seemed unstoppable, had been stopped, at least for the moment.

Deeper trends seemed to be at work. Gays and lesbians simply refused to be shoved back into the closet. And by and large, unless whipped up by horror stories about child molesting, Americans seemed willing to accept them, tentatively perhaps, and a bit fearfully, but accept them nevertheless. Surveys of young people showed that a solid majority no longer believed that same-sex relations between consenting adults was "morally wrong."

Thus, as the 1980s dawned, gays and lesbians throughout America, and throughout the Western world, had reason to be optimistic about the future.

There was one small but troubling cloud on the horizon. It wasn't political, it was medical. A growing number of gay men were dying of otherwise nonfatal diseases. The problem appeared to be linked to a mysterious destruction of the body's immune system that was afflicting gay men. This was quickly to become the greatest peril facing the gay community in modern times.

8
The AIDS Epidemic and the Future

Today everyone has heard of AIDS—Acquired Immune Deficiency Syndrome. While not everyone knows exactly what AIDS is, they know this much: It is a deadly disease that up to this time has struck primarily gay men in America.

It came on very quickly. Back in 1983 no one really knew what AIDS was. It didn't even have a name. All the doctors really knew was that a lot of gay men who should have been in the prime of life were coming down with diseases ranging from a rare form of skin cancer to a rare form of pneumonia. And they were dying. A few doctors and others who watched the development of the disease closely feared that a catastrophe was about to happen. Most other people—doctors, gays, journalists, and government officials—ignored the developing evidence. Unfortunately, those who feared the worst were right, except that it turned out to be even more horrible than they feared.

No one knows where AIDS started. The best guess is that it began somewhere in Central Africa. No one knows whether it is a new disease, the result of a recent mutation, or if it's an old disease that had existed in some isolated corner of the world and just recently broken out of its isolation and spread around the world.

Those are problems that medical historians may solve someday. This is what we know now:

Beginning around 1980, gay men, particularly in New York and San Francisco, began coming down with a puzzling and terrifying set of diseases. An early sign was strange purplish spots or lesions that appeared on a person's body. This was diagnosed as Kaposi's sarcoma (KS). Kaposi's sarcoma was a rare form of skin cancer that usually appeared in elderly men. It had never been considered a dangerous form of cancer. People who got it would often live on for twenty or more years and then die of old age. In the early 1980s KS began appearing in young gay men, in a new and aggressively dangerous form.

There were a whole set of other dramatic and alarming symptoms. The end of this series of diseases was often *Pneumocystis carinii pneumonia*. This is a fatal disease, but before AIDS it was a rare one. The tiny protozoans that cause this form of pneumonia are everywhere, and they are usually held in check by the body's immune system. This form of pneumonia had previously appeared only among people who were poor and undernourished, lived in crowded and unsanitary conditions, and already had a series of illnesses. It was first recognized in the orphanages of postwar Europe. In the

1980s *Pneumocystis carinii pneumonia* was killing well-fed, affluent young men in their twenties and thirties—the sort of people who should have been in the prime of life and peak of health.

Doctors might be able to treat one disease successfully, but the patient would soon relapse or fall prey to another disease.

As the number of people with these puzzling symptoms multiplied it became clear that something was destroying the immune systems of these young men. But what? It took medical science several years to pin down the culprit, an infectious agent, a form of virus.

The AIDS virus was causing a devastating epidemic among gay men in the United States for a variety of reasons.

First, modern transportation facilitates the rapid spread of the AIDS virus, or any virus, throughout the world. It was possible at one time for a virus to be isolated among some small group in a remote part of the world for hundreds of years. This may have been true of the AIDS virus. But today there is no place that is completely remote.

The area of the world most severely affected by AIDS is Central Africa. The region is poor. Medical facilities are inadequate or nonexistent. No one really knows how long the disease has been present there, or how many people are dying from AIDS, but it's bad.

In the 1970s the Central African country of Zaire hired many better-educated Haitians to help administer the country. Zaire had once been a colony of Belgium. The Belgians spoke French, and when they were kicked out the rulers of the new indepen-

dent nation looked for French-speaking blacks who
could take over the role of the former colonial ad-
ministrators. Haitians, who speak French, seemed
an obvious choice. The Haitians may have picked up
the AIDS virus in Zaire and brought it back to their
homeland. Haitians were among the first in the
Western hemisphere to be afflicted with the disease.

Doctors who have studied the spread of AIDS
among gay men in the United States trace many of
the cases back to a gay French-Canadian airline
steward who was one of the earliest AIDS cases to
be diagnosed. Because of the nature of his job, the
steward had traveled widely in the United States,
Canada, and Europe. He may have picked up the
virus in Europe from someone who had been in one
of the French-speaking countries of Africa. He certainly spread the disease widely in the gay communities of the United States and Canada.

There is no single individual who can be blamed
for the disease. The virus could have reached the
United States in any one of a number of ways, and
there probably were several different avenues of
transmission. But twenty years earlier it would not
have spread so quickly.

The appearance of the AIDS virus coincided—cat-
astrophically, as it turned out—with the blossoming
of the gay liberation movement. Promiscuous, often
anonymous sex had always been part of the gay
world—not all of it, certainly, but a part. While gays
had to live hidden, underground lives it was hard to
establish any long-term relationships. Two single
men living together were always suspect. So there
were quick pickups in bars, parks, even public toi-

lets. No one knew anyone else's name. It was safest that way.

When gays were able to live more openly, this pattern of quick, anonymous sex with many different partners persisted and expanded. No only were there gay bars and clubs, there were also gay bathhouses, particularly in cities like New York and San Francisco where there were large gay populations. Despite the name, the bathhouses were not places where men went to get clean, they were commercial sex establishments. For a fee a man could rent a cubicle in one of the baths and then have sex with as many partners as his desire and energy allowed.

After years of being forced underground, suddenly liberated gays were behaving like drunken sailors on shore leave, or like drunken sailors on leave would have behaved if an unlimited number of sexual partners were available.

Not all gay men lived the promiscuous "fast track" life all the time. Many went to the baths only occasionally—when on vacation, for example. Others, particularly gays who did not live in large gay communities, lacked the opportunity or the desire for that sort of sex. Some gays positively disapproved of the baths and all anonymous sex as dehumanizing. But it is impossible to deny that during the 1970s and early 1980s some gay men had thousands of different sex partners, and others were very promiscuous.

Even before AIDS struck, many doctors who were either gay or sympathetic to gays were warning that a life built around the bathhouses was a medical disaster waiting to happen. Gays already had an alarmingly high incidence of venereal and other diseases related to sexual activity. These diseases were unpleasant and uncomfortable, but with modern medicine rarely deadly. They could be cured. Many of the newly liberated gay men felt that disease was a chance worth taking for sexual freedom. Besides, if they got something they could be cured with a shot or a pill.

Another reason that the AIDS virus became so widespread in the gay community before its deadly potential was recognized is that the disease has a long latency period. That means a person can be infected with the disease and show absolutely no symptoms at all for years. Because he looks and feels fine, he can go around having sex with others without the faintest notion that he is spreading a deadly disease.

Even after the evidence of AIDS became clear, many gays simply refused to believe it. They dismissed it as some sort of "media hype" or as exaggerations by people who hated homosexuals. For years gays had been told they were horrible people who did disgusting things they would be punished for. All the stories about AIDS sounded like another one of those warnings. The bathhouses were obviously centers for spreading the deadly disease, yet many in the gay community fought efforts to close them down. They denounced doctors and those gay leaders who warned them to change their life-styles. The truth was just too grim, and as many others have done throughout history, gays tried to deny the grim truth as long as possible. Then, as friends and lovers began getting sick and dying in great numbers, the truth of AIDS could be denied no longer.

If the gay community denied AIDS, many in the

larger society either ignored the disease or felt that "the perverts were getting what they deserved." The contrast between how the United States reacted to two different diseases is stark. In 1976 a small group of American Legionnaires attending a convention in Philadelphia were struck down with a serious and often fatal pneumonialike illness. Immediately after the outbreak, which was quite small, the U.S. government and medical authorities mobilized an enormous effort to find the cause of the disease and its cure. Newspapers and television gave the Legionnaires Disease extensive coverage. The cause was found quickly, and effective treatments were developed. In the face of the far greater threat of AIDS, reaction was slow and inadequate. It's impossible to escape the conclusion that had this been a disease that afflicted white, middle-class, heterosexual men, the reaction would have been much quicker, and thousands upon thousands of lives would have been saved. Americans also do not like to talk frankly and openly about sex or sexually transmitted diseases. This time silence was not golden. It was deadly.

The virus that causes the disease was discovered by French researchers in 1983. American researchers working along the same lines were also able to claim credit for the discovery of the AIDS virus. A test for infection with the virus was developed a short time after that. Even then some gays didn't want to take the test. They insisted it "proved nothing," and they feared that if they tested positive they might be shipped off to concentration camps. The fear sounds paranoid and exaggerated. Yet there were political and religious leaders, a minority, to be sure, but some quite influential, who called for quarantine of all who tested positive for the AIDS virus. One conservative columnist actually suggested that those who tested positive for the virus be tattooed, so that others could identify them immediately. That was reminiscent of the Nazi practice of tattooing prisoners in the death camps.

In 1985 the movie star Rock Hudson died of AIDS. Other prominent people had already died of the disease, or were suffering from it, but usually the nature of the illness was kept secret. Admitting AIDS also meant admitting homosexuality. Even Hudson denied the AIDS diagnosis until a few days before his death. In August 1984, after Hudson knew he had AIDS and had already gone to France to try to get treatment, he attended a state dinner at the White House. Hudson was a life-long Republican and an old Hollywood friend of Ronald and Nancy Reagan. Mrs. Reagan saw that Hudson had lost a lot of weight and looked ill. She asked about his health, and he told her that he had picked up some kind of flue bug while filming in Israel but that he was recovering and felt fine.

The announcement that Rock Hudson had died of AIDS caught the public attention like nothing else had. Not only was Rock Hudson a well-known film star, back in the 1950s and early 1960s he had been the symbol of handsome and healthy American masculinity. Rock Hudson and Doris Day were supposed to be the perfect pre-sexual revolution American couple. Hudson's friends knew he was gay. His millions of fans didn't. When it was revealed that Rock Hudson was not only gay but dying of a disease perceived as being a "gay plague," public discussion of AIDS moved to an entirely new level. Finally everybody paid attention.

At first there was a certain amount of AIDS hysteria. People outside of the gay community who didn't know much about the disease were terrified that they somehow might catch AIDS from the air, from a toilet seat, or from a handshake. The AIDS virus itself was portrayed in the press and on TV as a mysterious "supergerm."

None of this is true. There is nothing mysterious about the AIDS virus or how it works. Once French researchers were able to focus on the problem it took them less than a year to locate the virus.

There is no cure or vaccine for the disease. Viral diseases are notoriously difficult to cure or to protect against. The common cold is caused by a virus, and there is no cure and no effective vaccine.

What makes the AIDS virus so terrifying is that once it infects a person its progress is inexorable and deadly. Science does not yet know whether all people with the virus will eventually suffer so much damage to their immune systems that they will die from some AIDS-related disease, but right now it looks that way.

AIDS, however, is not easy to catch. The AIDS virus is transmitted by bodily fluids—that means primarily semen and blood. Small quantities of the virus have also been detected in tears and saliva, but in minute quantities. All the evidence indicates that in order to catch AIDS a person must receive a massive dose of the virus.

Early in the epidemic the virus was spread through blood transfusions, as infected people unknowingly donated blood that contained the virus.

Many in the gay community were very civic-minded and so they donated a lot of blood. When the infected blood was given to someone else they would also get the virus and eventually, in most cases, the disease. The test for AIDS antibodies, commonly called the "AIDS test," has all but eliminated this danger. All donated blood is screened for AIDS, as it is for a number of other diseases. Getting a blood transfusion in America today is safe.

There was a lot of confusion and misinformation about AIDS in the blood supply. One thing we must make clear is that there is absolutely no danger of infection when donating blood, and there never has been.

The disease spread rapidly through the gay community primarily through anal intercourse. This often produces tears in the tissue and thus the virus can be introduced directly into the bloodstream. Oral sex also has a potential for spreading the disease, particularly through any sort of sore or cut in the mouth. Many in the gay community were exceptionally vulnerable because they had already suffered from venereal diseases that produced sores through which the AIDS virus could enter their bodies.

AIDS is a horrifying disease, but not a mysterious or unnatural one.

There are no cheerful or optimistic conclusions that can be drawn from the AIDS crisis. But there have been some surprising developments. First, there is the reaction of the gay community itself. In the eyes of their detractors, gays are a bunch of sinful, hedonistic sickos. Yet once the real magnitude of the disease was realized the gay community did not dissolve, it pulled together. In addition to pursuing vigorous political action to get the government to put more money into AIDS research and treatment, it created an impressive network of education and self-help groups. Gay men who once spent their time on the beach or in the gym now spend hours in hospitals doing volunteer work with the sick and dying.

The political relations between lesbians and gay men had not always been smooth but in the face of the crisis lesbians responded. One of the many projects was the Blood Sister Project of San Diego, which enlisted hundreds of lesbians to donate blood that could then be used to help AIDS patients. Lesbians are one of the groups in the country with the lowest incidence of AIDS or any other sexually transmitted diseases. If AIDS is punishment for homosexual activity, does that mean that female homosexual activity is okay?

In his impassioned and shattering book, *And The Band Played On*, the story of the AIDS epidemic, Randy Shilts describes the scene and the mood at Gay Freedom Day in San Francisco in 1985, five years after the AIDS epidemic began.

"It was clear that the entire gay community also had something to share with the larger society. Hopeful Americans could learn from the gay community's mistakes and not waste valuable time floundering in denial; perhaps Americans could learn from the gay community's new strengths, as well. It was a far different vision of strength than what gays had imagined they would fashion when they marched proudly in the 1980 Gay Freedom Day Parade. The outward push for power contin-

ued, but it was largely eclipsed by the inward struggle for grit in the face of some of the cruelest blows
that fate had meted out to any American community. As gay people had helped each other find this
strength, they had forged a gay community that was
truly a community, not just a neighborhood. And by
now, there was also a shared sense that they wanted
the dream to survive. It had been a painful and difficult five years to reach this point, but it had come
this day.''

Perhaps the greatest surprise is that the AIDS epidemic didn't produce the sort of anti-gay backlash
that practically everyone expected. Sure, at first
there was some hysteria. There was some upsurge
in ''gay bashing''—violence against homosexuals.
The excuse of the bashers was that gays were
spreading AIDS and should be punished or killed.
But people who commit that sort of violence will
always find an excuse.

Says Shilts, ''For all the new rhetoric AIDS gave
to the old foes of homosexuals, it was clear that the
disease was making the gay community few new enemies; rather, people were coming to understand
the value of a gay person's life and the great injus-
tice that had been committed against gay people in
the course of the epidemic.''

Members of the gay community and their friends
have stitched together a gigantic quilt with thousands of panels, each containing the name of a
friend, a lover, a child who has died from AIDS. The
quilt has toured cities throughout the world and always attracts huge and emotional crowds. Few, gay
or straight, who have viewed it are not moved to
tears.

Where does the AIDS epidemic stand today? There is no cure for the disease nor is one likely in the near future. And there may never be a cure. (By cure we mean that the virus is entirely eliminated from a victim's body.) As we said, viral diseases are extremely difficult to cure. Tens of thousands of people now infected with the AIDS virus will probably die because of it.

Chances are far better that the disease can be successfully treated and managed. That is, the virus will remain in a person's body, but there will be drugs that will suppress or slow its destruction of the immune system and allow a person to live a longer and more normal life. Even that is no more than a hope right now. There is one drug, AZT, now in use in the United States that has successfully prolonged the lives of some AIDS sufferers, and there are many other drugs being developed both here and in other countries. A major complaint of AIDS groups is that the U.S. government is not moving quickly enough to get these drugs out to people who need them. And there is the constant complaint that not enough is being spent on research for new treatments. Right now people are dying who might be saved.

Many of those infected with the AIDS virus or friends of those who are infected have become quite desperate, and this desperation has driven them to dramatic and sometimes violent street demonstrations. The group called ACT UP has staged its demonstrations in front of the White House, in churches, at medical conferences, and many other places. They have attracted an enormous amount of publicity, much of it hostile. The effectiveness of such demonstrations in changing people's minds is unknown. But the members of ACT UP say that many are dying and being ignored, and they have no choice. If onlookers are offended, so be it.

A vaccine to prevent being infected by the virus is a possibility, but not an immediate one. At present the only way to prevent AIDS is to avoid being infected. And for gays the only way to do that is to radically alter sexual behavior. That means not having promiscuous, anonymous sex with dozens and perhaps hundreds of strangers. And it means using condoms all the time. Anyone who takes chances with AIDS, assuming science will find a cure before they get sick, is crazy.

This safe-sex message seems to have gotten out. The rate of new AIDS infections among gays appears to have dropped dramatically. That does not mean the epidemic is over among gays. Tens of thousands are still infected, tens of thousands will still die. For years the death rate from AIDS will go up, not down. But even without dramatic new treatments, doctors who study epidemics look forward to the day when the death rate, too, will begin to decline, so long as gays don't go back to the free and easy pre-AIDS sexual behavior.

Scientists are now turning their attention to another threatened segment of American society, intravenous (IV) drug users. IV drug users often share needles, and in so doing share the AIDS virus. A small amount of AIDS-infected blood remains in the needle. The disease is spreading more quickly among drug users than in any other segment of the population. It also spreads to the sexual partners of drug users, and to their children. An AIDS-infected mother will pass the virus on to her infant. It's much much harder to get the message about the dangers of AIDS out to the drug users than it was to warn the gay community.

For a time there was talk of an "explosion" of AIDS in the non-drug-using heterosexual population. In Africa the disease seems to be spread primarily through heterosexual sex. But there has been no explosion of AIDS among heterosexuals in America. The disease has been spreading, slowly, but mainly among the partners of IV drug users, and that means mainly among the poor in the inner cities.

Why has the pattern of AIDS infection been so different in America than in Africa? No one knows for sure. The best guess is that in Africa, where people are often poor, malnourished, and without adequate (or often any) medical care, they fall victim to a large number of other diseases, many of which can cause genital lesions or sores through which the AIDS virus can get into the bloodstream. These diseases are also more common among the poor inner city dwellers in America who are getting the disease through heterosexual sex.

Right now, for Americans who are not the partners of IV drug users, the risk of getting AIDS through heterosexual sex is small. Please note that we said the risk is small, not that there is no risk at all. There very definitely *is* a risk. Anyone engaging in casual or promiscuous and unprotected sex is playing Russian roulette. You may get away with it. But the virus is out there, and if you make an unlucky choice it can kill you. At the very least use a condom. It reduces the chance of heterosexually transmitted AIDS from small to even smaller.

For the gay teen the risk of AIDS is infinitely greater because there are so many infected people in the gay community. Most gay teens are aware of the risks. They worry about AIDS, but they are not overwhelmed by the fear of it. They feel that they can protect themselves by practicing safe sex. Studies have shown that it is much easier for young gays to accept the new and far more restrained sexual behavior forced on them by AIDS than it was for older gays, who had become accustomed to a different way of living. Young gays think about long-term relationships rather than a hot night at the baths or bar. They are looking for friendship and romance and not just sex. And, of course, they all know about condoms, something the previous generation of gay men never thought they would have to worry about.

Brian, a confident and optimistic young gay man, says that he is glad that he had come of age and come out after the AIDS threat had been realized. "If I was ten years older I'd probably be dead or dying by now. But now I take precautions. I know about safe sex. Sure I think about AIDS, but it doesn't dominate my life. My generation isn't infected, and it isn't going to be."

Is Brian right? We certainly hope so. But there are some troubling signs that young gays think that AIDS is now ancient history, something that just happened to older guys.

The Hetrick-Martin Institute is an organization that deals with young lesbians and gays. In a recent newsletter the Institute noted, "When it was announced that AIDS would be the subject of a weekly discussion . . . to which 50 young people usually came—a total of two clients showed up. . . . AIDS, with its associations with sickness, death, and modified sexual behavior, is an off-putting topic."

The newsletter goes on to say that teens—all teens, not just gay teens—have a sense of invulnerability, "the feeling that one can drive a car at 120 mph without risking anything, for instance." There is also the feeling that now is forever, and tomorrow will never come.

Besides young gays often don't know anybody who has died of AIDS or is suffering through the tortures of the disease. That does not mean that they don't know anybody who is carrying the virus and can infect them. "The people that they might know who have full-blown AIDS are 'old'—in their mid- to late twenties," the Institute newsletter says.

The gay teen who has come out and is a member of one of the many gay groups is bound to be bombarded with accurate information about the dangers of AIDS and what safe sex really means. He won't be able to avoid the subject. The danger may be greatest for the closeted and isolated gay teen, who has to rely on the preachy and inadequate information that he gets through school, or on the "common knowledge" that is picked up on the street or in gay bars. That sort of "knowledge" can kill.

9 *Growing Up Gay*

"At boarding school when they found the *Playboy* pictures they gave me my own room." —CHERYL S., AGE 18

"I'm having a secret affair with the president of my fraternity at college. If you're in a fraternity, people just don't think you're gay." —KENNETH B., AGE 19

What's it like to be a gay or lesbian teen in America today? It can be brutal or not so bad, and it can have wonderful moments. There is no such thing as a typical or average experience. Every life is unique.

What follows in this chapter are excerpts from interviews with eleven gay and lesbian teens. The names and some of the identifying details have been altered to protect individual identities. Unfortunately, that's necessary. The words and stories are absolutely authentic.

MICHAEL What's the best word to describe Michael? Ordinary, at least on the surface. He's the kind of person who can walk through a crowd without being noticed. Going unnoticed is useful when you're a teenager who's gay. The place where Michael lives is ordinary, too, a middle-class New Jersey suburb with the usual shopping malls, fast-food restaurants, and small houses with well-mowed lawns and neat backyards.

"I came out to myself in ninth grade when I was fourteen. So what? I knew I was attracted to boys instead of girls but what did I really know about being gay? Nothing! There had to be other boys who liked boys—I go to a big school—but who were they? I'd heard rumors some of the teachers were gay—but who? My guidance counselor was the kind of person you went to for a schedule change. You'd never talk about sex with her."

Michael didn't dare come out to his parents. "I didn't talk to them about anything serious or important in ninth grade, certainly not this." Knowing his mother, Michael assumed the first words out of her mouth would be, "What if your relatives find out?" And Michael had to admit to himself that coming out to his large close-knit Jewish family would not be fun.

"My relatives live for bar mitzvahs and weddings. Crazy as it sounds, I used to worry about what would happen to me when I got old enough to get married. My aunts are always talking about who's going to get married next and who's going to give what present and after the wedding who's going to give the first baby shower. Can't you just see me saying, 'Hey, Aunts, I'm gay!' Somehow I don't think they'd plan a big wedding celebration for me and my lover." Michael realized his safe niche in the family was gone. "I didn't fit in anymore." It was a lonely feeling.

He was under a lot of stress. For years Michael had dreamed of becoming an architect, and his room was cluttered with plans he'd designed of fantastic buildings straight out of the sci-fi stories he loved to read. But as early as tenth grade he was too drained, too worried, too confused, and too lonesome to be creative. He stopped designing buildings.

"In eleventh grade I got an after-school job at the public library where I came across a book called *One Teenager in Ten*, life histories of gay teens. I was afraid to sign it out—I didn't want the librarians to know I was reading it—so I stole it. Reading the book, I felt tremendously relieved just to know there were other gay teens out there."

Michael had made friends with four girls at school. He found them easy to talk to, but was it safe to come out to them? "I asked them to meet me for pizza and I said, 'I have something to tell you. But visualize my suicide if you ever tell anyone else.'"

The girls did not betray him, so he decided to come out to a boy he'd known for years. "Joshua goes to another school. He's straight, he's an athlete. I knew I'd never have the courage to tell him if I saw him, and I didn't even want to tell him on the phone." So Michael wrote Joshua a nine-page letter. "I began by hinting that I was gay. Not until the end of the letter did I just come out and say it."

Joshua responded well, as the girls had, and this gave Michael the strength to come out to his mother. Her first words? "What if your relatives find out?" At least Michael had known what to expect. "I said my happiness should be more important to her than the opinions of our relatives. She seemed to understand. We had a long talk. It was very meaningful. Or at least I thought it was. But since that talk every time I say anything about being gay she changes the subject. She treats my homosexuality as if it's hush-hush."

It was now June and time for the next big family wedding. "My mother begged me to bring a girl as my date. But I took my boyfriend to the wedding. I didn't announce, 'Look, Aunts, here's the person I'm in love with.' But if they guessed, so what?"

Michael's back to designing buildings straight out of science fiction again.

VICKI   Vicki grew up in a small town in Iowa not far from Des Moines. Her childhood was like a million other midwestern childhoods. She was a member of 4-H, raised dogs, rode horses, went to the Methodist Church, and played the flute in the junior high school band. She's on the girl's track team in high school. This is her senior year.

"I had crushes on girls in junior high. That scared me. Then I read an article in a magazine that said teenagers who are attracted to their own sex are just going through a phase. So I beat down my sexual fantasies and told myself everything would be okay. One magic morning I'd wake up straight, get married, and have kids. If I hadn't fallen in love with Tammy this year I might still believe I was just going through a gay phase, that I could float my way right into marriage expecting I'd turn out straight. Now I know better. I'm not going to 'turn' anything. I am gay.

"In September B.T. (Before Tammy) I had my first and only boyfriend. Having a boyfriend was very reassuring. Now I was like all the other girls. But after a couple of months I could tell something was wrong. I felt guilty even just kissing my boyfriend and I never went much further with him. I don't feel any guilt when I have sex with Tammy.

"She moved to town around Thanksgiving. After we became friends I felt deeper feelings for her than I'd ever felt for my boyfriend, so I broke up with him. The way Tammy and I feel about each other is more than sexual. I'm closer to her than I've ever been to anybody. She's beautiful and I love her."

TOM In the West where Tom lives, a land of ranches and mountains, nobody would ever guess he was gay. Nobody would dare dream of such a thing. Not Tom. High school football star. Good basketball player. Tom rides horses. Tom ropes calves. Strong, masculine-looking athletes like Tom just can't be gay.

"When I was in sixth grade the teacher asked us to write about a special friend so I wrote about my best friend Greg." There was nothing sexual about the story, but Tom enjoyed weaving a fantasy about spending time with Greg fishing, bowling, going to movies. It was a happy story. In a way it was a love story, though Tom didn't see it that way at the time.

By high school, "I was dating the same girls Greg dated." Lots of girls wanted to go out with Tom, "but until they went out with Greg I wasn't interested in them." Then one Friday night "Greg and I went out drinking. Usually there were other guys with us. Not that night. I wrestled with Greg—pretended I was kidding around—and I took his shirt off. Nothing happened, but Greg's straight and he must have sensed something because he pulled away, quickly put his shirt back on, and left. Next day I apologized and explained everything away by saying I'd been drunk. Greg accepted this and said not to worry about it.

"Over Christmas vacation, Paul, a guy I'd known all my life but never liked very much, came home from college. He asked me to take a drive with him. I didn't have anything else to do so I went. He came out to me and asked me if I was gay, too. I'd never put a name to what I felt, but when he said that word 'gay' everything fell into place. Things I hadn't understood suddenly made sense. Even though I wasn't really attracted to him we made love. It was very different from being with a girl and a whole lot better. After it was over I felt peaceful. I'd never felt peaceful after sex with a girl.

"I'm not going to hang around this little town much longer. I've got to move to a big city where there's a future for me as a gay man."

JULIA   In her sophomore year Julia had the reputation of being a notorious boy chaser. "But this was all show. What I did was have serious, passionate relationships with guys who live in another state —Connecticut. That's where my father is. My parents are divorced and I live with my mother in Los Angeles. That means my relationships with boys happened mostly over the phone. But pretending to my friends that I was crazy about boys—even though the boys were far away—convinced everybody that I was strongly attracted to guys. I was so convincing at this little game that when I came out to my friends they refused to believe I was gay and swore I had to be bisexual."

But Julia's "little game" did more than fool her friends. For a long time it allowed Julia to fool herself. Julia is now sixteen and in eleventh grade. "Up to this year I wouldn't admit to myself how strongly I was attracted to women, even though whenever I went out with a boy for any length of time I always broke up with him. But the word gay frightened me. I couldn't be that word, 'gay.' I used to buy *Playboy* just to look at the pictures of women and still didn't connect. Yet I was always comfortable with girls and now find kissing my girlfriend the most natural thing in the world."

Julia's lucky to live in a city with a large gay community. "I've always had a life outside high school. I'm active in the anti-nuclear movement, and at a peace seminar I met two older women who sensed I was gay. They invited me over for dinner, told me they were lesbians, and encouraged me to talk about my feelings. They were very happy together and I said to myself, 'Maybe being gay isn't so bad after all.' They introduced me to younger lesbians and I sort of glided into coming out. Now I'm very active in gay youth organizations and I've been working for gay rights."

Julia's out to a lot of people at her school. "I go to a big school. It's about seventy-five percent black. Black kids and white kids go their own way. The black kids don't care if I'm gay. The white kids put up with me because I'm white. I'm not worried about being harassed. It's mostly effeminate boys

who are harassed. I know how to protect myself.
I'm strong and I've been learning karate.

"I'm out to my mother. At first she blamed herself
for making me 'this way.' Now she doesn't. But I
won't tell my father and stepmother. My father
would use my homosexuality as a weapon against
my mother. He might go to court and try to get me
away from her. I find that very scary and it also
makes me very mad!"

ERIC Eric, who lives in Ohio, describes himself
as "the wimpy type. I got beat up and pushed
around in junior high and high school, but not because anyone suspected I was gay. Wimps get beat
up." Eric is being hard on himself. Actually, he's an
easygoing, pleasant-looking person with a pleasing
personality.

He wasn't even upset when kids called him a
"faggot." "I'd just say it back. It didn't mean anything but strange or weird." Perhaps the name-calling would have bothered him more if he'd related
his being attracted to boys to being gay. "But I
didn't. I didn't say 'I'm gay' to myself until I was a
senior. Before my senior year I went out with girls,
but only girls who went to other schools. I didn't
want to go out with a girl from my own school because I'd have to see her every day."

Not only the girls he went out with but his two
best friends went to other schools. They were a boy
and a girl who worked with him at a supermarket
after school and on Saturdays. "I came out to the
girl first because I thought she could listen better.
She was nice when I told her, but she was sure I
could change if I got counseling. She told me I

should fight back. I didn't have to be gay. I should give girls a chance. She kept pushing me to go to my senior prom so I asked a girl and went. I wish I'd stayed home."

Eric's other friend, Jim, was embarrassed when Eric came out to him. He avoided Eric as much as he could and eventually broke off their friendship. Eric was so hurt he quit his supermarket job.

Next, he wrestled with ways to tell his parents. He never did come out to them—exactly. On his eighteenth birthday his mother found a box of pamphlets, magazine articles, etc., about gays. She asked him point-blank if he was gay. He didn't answer, which she took to mean yes, and she shouted, "We don't want you living here." There was a huge fight with everybody screaming at everybody else. His sixteen-year-old sister burst into tears. His father blamed his mother. Eric rushed upstairs to his room and packed his clothes. His mother relented and told him that since it was his birthday he could stay the night. But it was too late. "I said no, I'm leaving. I'll pick up the rest of my stuff later.

"I drove around for a long time. I didn't know what to do or where to go. I felt terrible. I'd met a gay guy at a bar who had his own apartment. I really didn't want to go there because I hadn't had sex with anybody yet and I was scared he'd expect me to become his lover if I stayed with him. He was older than me and he'd been with a lot of men and I wasn't ready for that. But when it got late I phoned him and went to his place. And we did become lovers but I was real unhappy, so two weeks later I went back home. But my family acted like I was a werewolf or something, so as soon as I graduated I got my own apartment and went to work full-time in a restaurant.

"At the restaurant I came out to a couple of straight people in their twenties." And Eric learned a sad lesson. "Straight people may accept your being gay, but only as long as you don't talk about it. Even when they don't hassle you they don't want to hear about your boyfriends or your life. They won't even try to understand what being gay is all about."

Eric doesn't know who he can trust anymore.

JODI Ask Jodi to describe herself and here's what she says: "I look like a boy. I keep my hair very short and I only wear a skirt or dress when I absolutely have to. When I was little I was such a tomboy I never played with girls. All my friends were boys. Now I only want to be with girls. Not that I'm out at school—I'm not that gutsy—but because of the way I look every once in a while someone will make jokes about gays on purpose as I walk by, making sure I hear. But it's because of me that our girls' softball team won the state championship last year. I pitched a no-hitter. So nobody hassles me, and I was even voted president of the student council this year."

Jodi has always loved team sports. She likes the excitement they bring, the intensity, the competition. But she also likes team sports because "they allow you to be with girls when boys aren't around and when girls haven't got boys on their mind. When girls get together in a group outside of athletics they spend most of their time talking about who they're going out with and what kind of clothes boys like girls to wear. That's not for me."

Jodi, a senior, first sensed she was gay in seventh grade. "I had a teacher in junior high—I'm sure she was gay—who kept staring at me. I think she was trying to reach out to me, to help me, but she was probably afraid to say anything because she might get into trouble.

"I came out to myself in ninth grade when I fell in love with my best friend. But I was afraid to say anything to her because she was straight. I couldn't even come out to girls I wasn't attracted to because what if they thought I was coming on to them? There are other lesbians at school—there's got to be —but we're all too afraid to make the first move. Not that I care anymore, because a couple of months ago I overheard some college students joking about how they'd gone 'sightseeing' at the local gay bar. Now that I knew the name of the bar I drove there to check it out. I was scared but I went inside anyway. A girl asked me to dance and when the dance was over she took me to a lesbian bar."

Jodi found the lesbian bar more relaxed and comfortable than the other bar, which was tense and frenzied and primarily for gay men. "I go back to the lesbian bar as often as I can, though I worry that someone I know will see me there and tell my parents or the coach. So far that hasn't happened and graduation is only a few weeks away. Only lesbians seem to know where lesbian bars are. Even cab drivers can't tell you where to find them."

It was at the bar that Jodi met her girlfriend, Jean. Jean's at the state college on an athletic scholarship. Guess where Jodi's going to be next fall?

* * *

ANDY Andy, eighteen, doesn't live with his mother anymore. He's staying with a family that takes in gay teens who've been kicked out of their homes. "I came out to my mother two years ago in the middle of a fight and she got so mad she kept hitting me. She wouldn't stop, so I ran out of the apartment to the 7-Eleven store and called the police. They got social services involved and I was put in a temporary home and given counseling. From then on it was back and forth between shelters and temporary homes until I turned eighteen and moved in with Barry and Joan. They've got a son—he's a doctor in Philadelphia—who's gay and they're very understanding.

"I had gay feelings when I was five or six and by eighth grade I felt different inside from everybody I knew and the kids called me a fag. Eighth grade is when my mother began nagging me and picking on me, too, because by then I was noticeably effeminate and she probably suspected I was gay and hated me for it. She treated me like I was the little maid around the house. She made me clean up all the time. She never stopped complaining about me. She'd tell me to get my act together, to be more like a man.

"Eighth grade was also when phys ed became worse than math class. Not that I got sexually aroused in the gym or locker room. I was too scared for that to happen. But there's a locker room mentality that's very intimidating if you're gay. There are no teachers in the locker room and coaches are terrible. To fit in I tried to play soccer but the coach wouldn't let me. He called me a 'sissy' in front of everybody and made me sit on the bench. Every-

body laughed. It was humiliating. Coaches have
taught me just how unkind people can be. Even
class trips and school dances are bad for me because there isn't much adult supervision and when
there isn't much supervision students are carefree
and rambunctious and ready to go gay bashing. Before class trips my knees start shaking, I get so
scared.

"By the end of ninth grade the rumors were all
over school that I was gay even though I hadn't
done anything with anybody. To protect myself I
started telling people I was bi because it's safer to
be bi than gay, and I started working hard on looking and acting less effeminate. I'm always watching
every gesture to control it.

"Now that I'm eighteen things are a lot better.
The rumors that used to scare off straight friends
have less effect now. My friends (they're practically
all girls) seem to listen to me more than the rumors.
I think it's just that people won't see you're gay if
they like you.

"At the beginning of the year I started making eye
contact with boys and girls in my class who are also
gay. Up to now we've been too frightened to hang
around together. Now and only now that we're going to graduate soon are we becoming friends."

ALLYSON Allyson, seventeen, is tall and wil-
lowy and has long, red hair. She's very pretty and
classically feminine in appearance. There's never
been a hint of the tomboy about her. She plays the
piano and takes art lessons. And though she hasn't
had any sexual experience she knows she's gay.

Because Allyson didn't want to be different from

the other students at her affluent suburban New England high school, she came out to herself gradually. "In ninth grade I had my first and only opposite-sex crush. I belong to a Unitarian Church youth group—my church is very tolerant—and there used to be a boy in the group who was openly gay. He would wear buttons that said 'Gay and Proud' to meetings and he was a volunteer for the gay hot line. I was very shy around him and we never talked but I thought he was wonderful. Perhaps the reason I had a crush on him was because he was openly expressing what I was secretly feeling."

In her sophomore year Allyson made friends with a straight girl named Gail. "I became her satellite, dying my hair and piercing four holes in my ears because that's what she did. I was obsessed with her. Even her annoying traits, her faults, preyed on my mind. I didn't say to myself, 'I love this person,' but after we drifted into new friendships I wondered at the intensity of my feelings toward her. It was during the time I knew Gail that I first became aware that all I can feel for boys is friendship.

"I came out to myself completely last summer when I was a counselor-in-training at a summer camp. I was staring at a girl—a counselor—I found particularly attractive when a boy—a college student who worked at the camp and who was watching me watch her—asked me in a friendly way if I was gay. To my utter amazement, instead of saying no I said 'maybe.' I had never admitted this much to myself before, and I knew as soon as I said 'maybe' that what I really meant was yes.

"After the summer was over I went crazy worrying about whether I should tell my parents or not. I tried several times to come out to them but I'd just choke up. Then over Christmas vacation I went to visit my aunt in Seattle, because I'm thinking of going to college on the West Coast and I wanted to look around. Well, I deliberately went to a women's bookstore to meet lesbians, and when I did we explored the gay community together. I met a lot of women. Some of the lesbians I liked, but some were as bad as straight boys who are just looking for a quick pickup. I want a trusting, monogamous relationship. The day before I came home I met two lesbians who considered themselves married and that made me feel a lot better. And meeting so many lesbians made me very conscious of how deeply gay I am."

That certainty gave Allyson the courage to come out to her parents the day she came home.

SCOTT "Sometimes I see a girl I might be capable of having sex with but I'd probably leave her in a minute for a guy, and if I ever did get into bed with a girl I couldn't have an orgasm unless I pretended she was a boy." That's Scott (now a freshman in college) speaking. Yet in high school he had everybody fooled. He had the reputation of being cute and shy, awkward but likable, and very definitely straight. To make sure everybody thought he was straight he hung around with the most aggressive anti-gay jocks in the school.

"I kept as far away as I could from the effeminate boys everybody was sure were gay. They were what I didn't want to be. I wasn't about to be lumped with anybody who drew the shout 'faggot.' " Besides providing cover, the jock crowd appealed to

Scott because they went to a lot of parties and had a good time. He didn't join in when they baited effeminate boys or told jokes about "queers." He just looked the other way and shrugged.

Until senior year. That's when Scott discovered the gay bar in the next town and got to know Kevin. Kevin was from one of the poorest families in Scott's town. Scott's family went to the Presbyterian Church. Kevin's family had never been inside any church. Scott's family owned a dry cleaner's. Kevin's family was on welfare. Scott dressed conservatively. Kevin looked like an escapee from a second-rate heavy metal band and zoomed around town on a motorcycle. He was also as openly gay as anyone can possibly be in a small rural community.

Kevin became Scott's first lover. "He was honest and he was free. That's what I liked about him. He knew who my friends were and he asked me why I hung around with those guys. He told me, 'Any friend who can't accept you as gay isn't a friend.' But I was still afraid to come out to anyone I knew. It was rough, because now that I was completely out to myself I was bursting to tell. Well, I did come out right before graduation but in a crazy explosive way. I just couldn't take the pressure anymore."

On a Friday night in June Scott went to a party. He started drinking and kept on drinking. The school blabbermouth was at the party, a girl he'd known since second grade. She said, "I saw you talking to Kevin. Are you fooling around with him?" Scott could have lied. He could have come up with a half dozen excuses for talking to Kevin. Instead, he couldn't stop himself from saying yes. By Monday every teenager in the high school knew that Scott was gay.

It was good-bye, jocks. But if his old friends avoided him, at least they didn't call him names—not to his face, anyway. And he made some new friends. He graduated from high school, survived the summer, and went away to college. "I got away lucky. In tenth grade two girls were caught having a sexual encounter in the woods at the edge of town and they were driven out of school."

RORY   When Rory was a child he was gentle and sensitive and played with Barbie dolls, so boys rejected him. He had only one close friend, a girl. As he grew older his friends remained mostly girls "who were outcasts, too." Rory's father first began to worry about Rory when he was six, and he asked Rory's mother, Lynn, to take him to a doctor and "see if something's wrong with his hormones." Lynn was shocked. But a year later she, too, admitted to herself that Rory was already strikingly effeminate.

In kindergarten the other children made fun of Rory. He turned to his teacher for help but she seemed to think it was his own fault he was effeminate. She was the first in a long line of teachers to hold that view. Rory survived by trying to ignore the taunting children and hostile teachers, but as he grew older he became less passive. He fought back with words.

His family moved to a small college town when he was twelve, but if his parents expected the town to be kinder to their son than the city suburb where he was born they were mistaken. Farms surrounded the town and the farm kids beat Rory up whenever they wanted. His very first day in school somebody called him a "faggot" and pushed him down the stairs.

Enemy territory ended at the guidance counselor's office. The guidance counselor let Rory stay with her between classes so he didn't have to walk through the halls with the other teenagers. Very few people in high school were even passably nice to Rory.

By thirteen Rory knew he was gay, and at fourteen he came out to his mother. She took him to the nearest large city every Saturday because there was a church in the city which had opened its doors to gay teenagers. But Rory felt out of place with the other gay teens he met there because they were runaways or had been kicked out of their homes by their parents and were turning tricks on the street to survive.

At home Rory "hounded the gay student groups at the college to please take me in even though I was only in high school. I was so lonely. I tried to kill myself by swallowing sleeping pills but my mother found me in time and an ambulance rushed me to the hospital."

After the suicide attempt Rory's parents sent him to a small boarding school on the West Coast. There he seemed to blossom. "I came out to everybody. The kids were different from the kids I'd known before. Those who wouldn't accept me had to shut up because the other kids and the staff wouldn't tolerate persecution."

But there was to be no magical happily-ever-after for Rory. He had known too much pain. "I quit school at the end of my junior year and changed my name to Christopher. No more Rory. I'm eighteen now and I live in a city with a large gay community. I wear makeup. I change my hair color whenever I feel like it. I'm glad I'll never have children because I wouldn't want them growing up in this cruel society.

"Tell straight teenagers gayness is not a decision. Tell them it comes from within. Ask them to leave us alone."

JOEL In October, one month from his eighteenth birthday, Joel found himself in a roomful of gay guys his own age for the first time in his life and heard them saying things like, "Isn't John good looking?" or "Adam is cute." Instantly Joel knew he was where he belonged. It may have felt like paradise but in reality it was merely an ordinary meeting of the gay student group at his college.

"Even though I was attracted to boys more than girls in high school I wasn't really out to myself. To keep from thinking about sex I studied very hard and was the valedictorian of my class. But you can only lie to yourself so far. I hated listening to my friends—they were all girls—talk about boys because I couldn't join in. I couldn't say, 'Hey, Lisa, your boyfriend's good looking,' or giggle and point to a cute boy passing by and whisper, 'Isn't he gorgeous?'

"The first time I went out with a girl was last summer. She goes to college in Boston, too, so I continued seeing her in September. But being with her was so blah I got scared and I decided once and for all I'd prove to myself I was straight by going to a meeting of the gay students' organization on campus. I told myself that when I got there I'd know at once I didn't belong and I'd leave and find a girlfriend for real. Instead, I fell in love with a boy and walked out of the meeting with him.''

Since then being gay has been great. Joel and his boyfriend are having a wonderful time exploring Boston's lively gay community. They browse through gay bookstores together, go to restaurants where they meet other gays and talk for hours, take in gay theatrical productions, and go to concerts featuring gay musicians.

Coming out to his parents went smoothly for Joel, too. "I came out to them at Christmas vacation because my boyfriend was coming to stay with us over the holidays and he's very feminine-looking so I knew my parents would guess I was gay as soon as they met him. My mother said, 'It's no surprise,' when I told her I was gay. Then we shared a good laugh over several relatives in the family she's sure are gay. She wondered if I felt comfortable telling my father. I'd come out to her first because I think it's easier to talk to mothers than fathers. Fathers tend to have a 'nudge-nudge' attitude toward sex.

"But when I told my father he gave me a hug and said, 'I just want you to be happy.' I'm very lucky that my parents have given me the freedom to be openly gay."

ADDRESSES AND
PHONE NUMBERS

This is a book aimed at teens who want to know more about the lives of their gay and lesbian contemporaries and about homosexuality in general. We realize that it will also be read by some gay and lesbian teens or by teens who think they may be. What follows is a brief list of addresses and phone numbers from which you can obtain further information, or just find somebody to talk to about yourself, your friends, your relatives, or anything else relating to homosexuality. You can also get up-to-date information for reports.

P-Flag (Parents and Friends of Lesbians and Gays) is a nationwide organization with chapters in practically every state in the Union. The organization sponsors meetings and research projects, issues literature, and may provide speakers to organizations and schools or simply an understanding person to talk to. The address and phone number of local organizations can be obtained by writing to the main headquarters:

P-Flag
P.O. Box 20308, Denver, Colorado 80220

The largest and most active of the gay churches is:

The Universal Fellowship of Metropolitan
  Community Churches
5300 Santa Monica Blvd., Suite 304, Los Angeles,
  California 90029

For information on health-related matters, and to-day that usually means AIDS, write:

Gay Men's Health Crisis, Inc.
Box 274, 132 West 24th Street, New York, New York
  10011

The American Social Health Association has a 24-hour toll-free AIDS hot line. The number is:

800-342-2437

For more information on a wide variety of sub-jects relating to homosexuality, including a collec-tion of first-rate stories about gay teens in comic book form entitled *Tales of the Closet*, write:

Hetrick-Martin Institute
401 West Street, New York, New York 10014

For more immediate help and referrals there's the National Gay/Lesbian Crisisline.
Outside New York State phone 800-221-7044,

Monday through Friday, 5:00 P.M. to 10:00 P.M. Eastern Standard Time.

Within New York State phone 212-529-1604, Monday through Friday, 5:00 P.M. to 10:00 P.M.

If you phone before or after hours or on weekends there's an answering machine that will refer you to other numbers to call in case of emergency. The main numbers are often busy, so be patient.

BOOKS, FILMS, AND VIDEOS

What follows is a list of materials that are easily available and will help you understand lesbians and gays.

BOOKS

Brown, Rita Mae. *Rubyfruit Jungle*. New York: Bantam Books, 1973.
This famous novel about a bold, smart, adventurous lesbian named Mollie Bolt is fun to read.

Clark, Don. *Loving Someone Gay*. New York: Signet, 1977.
A guide for friends and relatives of gays, as well as gays themselves. This book is written by a gay therapist.

Colman, Hila. *Happily Ever After*. New York: Scholastic, 1986.

A young adult novel. Paul, seventeen, is gay. Only Melanie, sixteen, who loves him, doesn't know it. What happens when she finds out.

Fricke, Aaron. *Reflections of a Rock Lobster*. Boston: Alyson Publications, 1981.
The author, who is gay, took his boyfriend to his senior prom and wrote this book about it.

Garden, Nancy. *Annie On My Mind*. New York: Farrar, Straus and Giroux, 1982.
A beautiful, bittersweet love story about two teenage girls.

————. *Lark in the Morning*. New York: Farrar, Straus & Giraux, 1991.
The central character of this sensitive novel is also gay, but the author demonstrates that sexual orientation is not the only aspect of a gay teenager's life. The author shows that despite differences teens share many of the same reactions, thoughts, and feelings.

Gleitzman, Morris. *Two Weeks with the Queen*. New York: Putnam, 1991.
This book, with an English setting, is about a young Australian boy who is searching for the best doctor in London to help his brother, who is dying of cancer. He is sure the Queen will know, hence the title of the book. At the "Best Cancer Hospital in London" he meets and becomes friends with a young man whose lover is dying of AIDS. This is a lovely book for young readers who need to know about being gay and AIDS. And who doesn't?

Heron, Ann (editor). *One Teenager In Ten*. New York: Warner Books, 1983.
Though this collection of autobiographical accounts by gay teens is meant for other gay teens, straight readers will find the book enlightening and interesting.

Homes, A. M. *Jack*. New York: Macmillan, 1989.
A fifteen-year-old discovers that his divorced father is gay. The revelation provokes an emotional crisis.

Kerr, M. E. *Night Kites*. New York: Harper, 1987.
A high school boy learns that his beloved older brother has AIDS and is coming home.

Klein, Norma. *Now That You Know*. New York: Bantam Books, 1988.
A young adult novel. Nina, a ninth grader in New York City, is an only child whose parents are divorced. Her world turns upside down when her father tells her he's gay. Can she get past her anger and confusion?

———. *Learning How to Fall*. New York: Bantam, 1989.
Gay issues are not central to this book, but it does give a realistic and sympathetic portrait of a young man's lesbian mother and her life partner.

Shilts, Randy. *And The Band Played On*. New York: Penguin Books, 1987.
A thorough chronological investigation of the AIDS epidemic. This well-written book reads like fiction, but, alas, it is all too true.

Snyder, Anne. *The Truth About Alex*. New York: Signet, 1981.

A young adult novel. The star quarterback of the high school football team is straight. His best friend is gay. They get along just fine until the rumors start. You may have seen the HBO special based on this book, starring Scott Baio and Peter Spence.

FILMS AND VIDEOS

Another Country (1984). Director: Marek Kanievska. Stars: Rupert Everett, Colin Firth, Michael Jenn.

This movie about young Guy Burgess and Donald Maclean (who later became Russian spies) takes you inside the upper-class English school system.

The Boys in the Band (1970). Director: William Friedkin. Stars: Kenneth Nelson, Peter White.

This film version of Matt Crowley's ground-breaking play is a funny, sad, and thought-provoking glimpse into gay life in an earlier era.

Brideshead Revisited. Director: Charles Sturridge. Stars: Anthony Andrews, Jeremy Irons, Claire Bloom, Laurence Olivier.

The early episodes of this beautifully made television adaptation of Evelyn Waugh's novel present a romantic, even lyrical vision of a gay love affair.

La Cage Aux Folles, Part I (1979), *La Cage Aux Folles*, Part II (1981). Director: Edouard Molinar. Stars: Ugo Tognazzi, Michel Serrault.

These charming French films, which were the basis for the hit Broadway musical, are about an aging and lovable gay couple who own a nightclub featuring entertainers in drag. The films are available dubbed in English.

The Color Purple (1985). Director: Steven Spielberg. Stars: Danny Glover, Whoopi Goldberg, Margaret Avery, Oprah Winfrey.

At the heart of this saga, based on Alice Walker's Pulitzer Prize-winning novel, is a strong and positive lesbian relationship.

Consenting Adults (1985). Director: Gilbert Cates. Stars: Marlo Thomas, Martin Sheen.

The dramatic story of a family thrown into turmoil when a son tells his parents he's gay. Based on the 1975 novel by Laura Z. Hobson.

Desert Hearts (1985). Director: Donna Deitch. Stars: Helen Shaver, Patricia Charbonneau, Audra Lindley.

Set in Reno, Nevada, in the 1950s, this is a perceptive, sensitive drama about a staid, unhappy woman and a free-spirited young lesbian who teaches her to love.

Kiss of the Spider Woman (1985). Director: Hector Babenco. Stars: William Hurt, Raul Julia, Sonia Braga.

Hurt won an Academy Award for his portrayal of an effeminate gay film buff in love with the political prisoner who shares his jail cell.

Llana (1983). Director: John Sayles. Stars: Linda Griffiths, Jane Halleran.

A married woman with children falls in love with her female professor and her entire life changes. One of the best films about coming out ever made.

Maurice (1987). Director: James Ivory. Stars: James Wilby, Rupert Graves, Ben Kingsley.

Based on E.M. Forster's novel, this may just be the finest movie on homosexuality ever. Despite the historical setting, this beautifully written and directed film has a lot to say about the prejudice gays face in any era.

My Beautiful Laundrette (1985). Director: Stephen Frears. Stars: Gordon Warnecker, Daniel Day-Lewis, Saead Jaffrey.

A working-class white punk and a young Pakistani become lovers in a shabby London neighborhood.

Outrageous! (1977). Director: Richard Benner. Stars: Craig Russell, Hollis McLaren.

There's nothing outrageous about this terrific film, which tells the story of a friendship between a pregnant young woman and a kind, generous, loyal, and very witty drag queen.

Parting Glances (1986). Director: Bill Sherwood. Stars: Richard Ganoung, John Bolger, Steve Buscemi.

A sympathetic, touching, but not the least bit morbid account of a gay couple whose close friend is dying of AIDS.

Personal Best (1982). Director: Robert Towne. Stars: Mariel Hemingway, Scott Glenn, Patrice Donnelly.

Well-written and well-acted, this film is about two women athletes training for the 1980 Olympics who have a lesbian relationship.

The Rocky Horror Picture Show (1975). Director: Jim Sharmen. Stars: Tim Curry, Susan Sarandon.

This delightful musical horror spoof is every teenager's favorite campy cult film. The audience as well as the cast gets into the act.

Tidy Ending (1988). Director: Harvey Fierstein. Stars: Stockard Channing, Harvey Fierstein.

A woman whose husband died of AIDS confronts her husband's lover. A made-for-TV film excerpt from Fierstein's Broadway play.

The Times of Harvey Milk (1984). Director: Robert Epstein.

Harvey Milk was the first openly gay person ever elected to public office in the United States. A San Francisco city supervisor, he was assassinated while in office. This Academy Award-winning documentary explores his career, the murder, and the explosive effect his life and death had on the city's gay community.

To Be or Not to Be (1983). Director: Alan Johnson. Stars: Mel Brooks, Anne Bancroft.

A gay man is one of the central characters in this comic remake of a 1942 film about a Polish theater troupe trying to survive the Nazi invasion.

Torch Song Trilogy (1988). Director: Paul Bogart. Stars: Harvey Fierstein, Anne Bancroft, Matthew Broderick.

Fierstein adapted and stars in this film version of his funny, bittersweet, and extremely popular Broadway play.

Victor/Victoria (1982). Director: **Blake Edwards.**
Stars: **Julie Andrews, Robert Preston.**
An amusing comedy about a woman posing as a
man posing as a woman, to the delight of her gay
male friend.

Be True to Yourself. (1991)
This is a half-hour video in which two gay men
talk with Tucson, Arizona, teens about growing up
gay. The speakers are proud, unapologetic, and successful, and present a startling contrast to the way
in which gays are usually portrayed. Producers of
the film suggest that it be sent to high school counseling offices, local youth organizations, and public
access TV stations. It is available from 21st Century
News, 6655 N. Canyon Crest Drive, Suite 12272,
Tucson, Arizona (602) 577-1397.

Additional and continually updated information
about gay and lesbian subjects, particularly as they
relate to teens, can be obtained from the National
Office of P-Flag, P.O. Box 27605, Washington, D.C.
20038-7605. Phone (202) 638-4200. FAX (202) 347-
5323.
Practically any gay and lesbian book in print (and
many out of print) can be located by calling Lambda
Rising booksellers at their toll free number, 1-800-
621-6969.

HIGH SCHOOL HELP LINE
FICTION BIBLIOGRAPHY

BEING GAY

Block, Francesca Lia. *Weetzie Bat*. New York: HarperCollins, 1989; Harper Trophy, 1991.

———. *Witch Baby*. New York: HarperCollins, 1991.

Chabon, Michael. *The Mysteries of Pittsburgh*. New York: William Morrow, 1988; HarperCollins, 1989.

Chambers, Aidan. *Dance on My Grave*. New York: HarperCollins, 1982; Harper Perennial, 1983; Harper Keypoint, 1986.

Childress, Alice. *Those Other People*. New York: Putnam, 1989.

Donovan, John. *I'll Get There: It Better Be Worth the Trip*. New York: HarperCollins, 1969.

Garden, Nancy. *Annie on My Mind*. New York: Farrar, Straus and Giroux, 1982; Sunburst/Farrar, Straus and Giroux, 1984.

―――. *Lark in the Morning*. Farrar, Straus and Giroux, 1991.

Guy, Rosa. *Ruby*. New York: Dell, 1992.

Holland, Isabelle. *The Man Without a Face*. New York: HarperCollins, 1988; Harper Keypoint, 1987.

Homes, A. M. *Jack*. New York: Macmillan, 1989.

Kerr, M. E. *Night Kites*. New York: HarperCollins, 1986; Harper Trophy, 1987.

Koertge, Ron. *The Arizona Kid*. Boston: Joy Street/Little, Brown, 1988; New York: Avon, 1989.

L'Engle, Madeleine. *A House Like a Lotus*. New York: Farrar, Straus and Giroux, 1984; Dell, 1985.

Levy, Elizabeth. *Come Out Smiling*. New York: Delacorte, 1981.

Meyer, Carolyn. *Elliott and Win*. New York: Margaret K. McElderry/Macmillan, 1986; Collier/Macmillan, 1990.

Mosca, Frank. *All American Boys*. Boston: Alyson Publications, 1983.

Rinaldi, Ann. *The Good Side of My Heart*. New York: Holiday House, 1987.

Scoppettone, Sandra. *Trying Hard to Hear You*. New York: HarperCollins, 1974.

Snyder, Anne. *Counter Play*. New York: New American Library, 1981.

Sweeney, Joyce. *Face the Dragon*. New York: Delacorte, 1991.

Walker, Alice. *The Color Purple*. San Diego: Harcourt Brace Jovanovich, 1982; New York: Washington Square Press/Pocket Books, 1983; Pocket Books, 1983.

Wersba, Barbara. *Just Be Gorgeous*. New York: HarperCollins, 1988; Dell, 1991.

White, Edmund. *A Boy's Own Story*. New York: New American Library, 1983.

Wieler, Diana. *Bad Boy*. New York: Delacorte, 1992.

ALCOHOL

Bauer, Marion Dane. *Shelter from the Wind*. New York: Clarion/Houghton Mifflin, 1979.

Brooks, Bruce. *No Kidding*. New York: HarperCollins, 1989; Harper Keypoint, 1991.

Due, Linnea A. *High and Outside*. New York: HarperCollins, 1980; Bantam, 1988.

Fox, Paula. *The Moonlight Man*. New York: Bradbury Press/Macmillan, 1986; Dell, 1988.

Greene, Shep. *The Boy Who Drank Too Much*. New York: Dell, 1980.

Scoppettone, Sandra. *The Late Great Me*. New York: Bantam, 1984.

Snyder, Anne. *My Name Is Davy: I'm an Alcoholic*. New York: New American Library, 1986.

Wagner, Robin S. *Sarah T.: Portrait of a Teenage Alcoholic*. New York: Ballantine, 1986.

DRUGS

Childress, Alice. *A Hero Ain't Nothin' but a Sandwich*. Santa Barbara: Cornerstone Books/ABC-CLIO, 1989; Avon, 1974.

Hinton, S. E. *That Was Then, This Is Now*. New York: Viking, 1971; Dell, 1989.

Knapp, Paul E. *False Positive*. Nashville: Winston-Derek, 1990.

Kropp, Paul. *Dope Deal*. St. Paul: EMC, 1982.

Stoehr, Shelley. *Crosses*. New York: Delacorte, 1991.

Strasser, Todd. *Angel Dust Blues*. New York: Putnam, 1979; Dell, 1981.

RAPE

Abbey, Deirdre. *Shadows After Closing*. Salt Lake City: RWS Books, 1988.

Asher, Sandy. *Things Are Seldom What They Seem*. New York: Delacorte, 1983.

Butterworth, Emma. *As the Waltz Was Ending*. New York: Four Winds Press/Macmillan, 1982; Scholastic, 1985.

Dizenzo, Patricia. *Why Me? The Story of Jenny*. New York: Avon, 1976.

MacLean, John. *Mac*. Boston: Houghton Mifflin, 1987; New York: Avon, 1989.

Miklowitz, Gloria D. *Did You Hear What Happened to Andrea?* New York: Delacorte, 1979; Dell, 1986.

Peck, Richard. *Are You in the House Alone?* New York: Viking, 1976; Dell, 1989.

PARENTS

Bridgers, Sue Ellen. *Permanent Connections*. New York: HarperCollins, 1987; Harper Keypoint, 1988.

Bunn, Scott. *Just Hold On*. New York: Delacorte, 1982.

Cannon, A. E. *Amazing Gracie*. New York: Delacorte, 1991.

Carter, Alden. *Robodad*. New York: Putnam, 1991.

Christopher, John. *The Guardians*. New York: Collier/Macmillan, 1992.

Colman, Hila. *Weekend Sisters*. New York: William Morrow, 1985; Juniper/Fawcett, 1988.

Dana, Barbara. *Necessary Parties*. New York: HarperCollins, 1986; Bantam, 1991.

Danziger, Paula. *The Divorce Express*. New York: Delacorte, 1982; Dell, 1983; G. K. Hall/Macmillan, 1988 (large print edition).

Dumond, Michael. *Dad Is Leaving Home*. New York: Rosen Group, 1987.

Hall, Lynn. *The Leaving*. New York: Macmillan, 1980; Collier/Macmillan, 1988.

Kerr, M. E. *Little Little*. New York: HarperCollins, 1981; Bantam, 1986.

Klein, Norma. *It's Not What You Expect*. New York: Avon, 1976.

Mahy, Margaret. *The Catalogue of the Universe*. New York: Margaret K. McElderry/Macmillan, 1986; Scholastic, 1987; G.K. Hall/Macmillan, 1987 (large print edition).

Martin, Katherine. *Night Riding*. New York: Alfred A. Knopf, 1989.

Mazer, Harry. *The Dollar Man*. New York: Dell, 1975; Magnolia, MA: Peter Smith, 1974.

McFadden, Cyra. *Rain or Shine*. New York: Knopf, 1986; Vintage/Random House, 1987.

Mills, Claudia. *Boardwalk with Hotel*. New York: Bantam, 1986.

Naylor, Phyllis Reynolds. *The Year of the Gopher*. New York: Atheneum/Macmillan, 1987; Bantam, 1988.

Peck, Robert Newton. *A Day No Pigs Would Die*.

New York: Knopf, 1972; Dell, 1979; Santa Barbara: ABC-CLIO, 1987 (large print edition).

Platt, Kin. *The Boy Who Could Make Himself Disappear.* New York: Dell, 1971.

Rylant, Cynthia. *A Kindness.* New York: Orchard, 1988; Dell, 1990.

Schwartz, Joel L., Aidan McFarlane, and Ann McPherson. *Will the Nurse Make Me Take My Underwear Off?: And Other Mysteries of Life as Revealed by Eric Mason.* New York: Dell, 1990.

Steiner, Barbara. *Tessa.* New York: William Morrow, 1988.

Stolz, Mary. *Go and Catch a Flying Fish.* New York: HarperCollins, 1979.

Townsend, Sue. *The Secret Diary of Adrian Mole, Aged 13³/₄.* New York: Avon, 1984.

Willey, Margaret. *Finding David Dolores.* New York: HarperCollins, 1986.

STRESS

Bonham, Frank. *Durango Street.* New York: Dutton, 1967; Dell, 1972.

Childress, Alice. *Rainbow Jordan.* New York: Putnam, 1990; Avon, 1982.

Crutcher, Chris. *Chinese Handcuffs.* New York: Greenwillow/William Morrow 1989; Dell, 1991.

———. *The Crazy Horse Electric Game* New York: Greenwillow/William Morrow, 1987; Dell, 1988.

Dale, Mitz. *Round the Bend.* New York: Delacorte, 1991.

Franco, Marjorie. *Love in a Different Key.* Boston: Houghton Mifflin, 1983.

Guest, Judith. *Ordinary People*. New York: Viking, 1982; Ballantine, 1986.

Holland, Isabelle. *Heads You Win, Tails I Lose*. New York: Fawcett, 1988.

Levenkron, Steven. *The Best Little Girl in the World*. New York: Warner, 1989.

Mulford, Philippa G. *If It's Not Funny, Why Am I Laughing?* New York: Delacorte, 1982.

Myers, Walter Dean. *Fast Sam, Cool Clyde, and Stuff*. New York: Viking, 1975; Puffin/Viking Penguin, 1988.

Oneal, Zibby. *The Language of Goldfish*. New York: Viking, 1980; Puffin/Viking Penguin, 1990.

Peck, Richard. *Don't Look and It Won't Hurt*. New York: Dell, 1991.

Pfeffer, Susan Beth. *About David*. New York: Delacorte, 1980; Dell, 1982.

Sweeney, Joyce. *Right Behind the Rain*. New York: Delacorte, 1987; Dell, 1991.

Thomas, Joyce C. *Marked by Fire*. New York: Avon, 1982.

Zindel, Paul. *My Darling, My Hamburger*. New York: HarperCollins, 1969; Bantam, 1984.